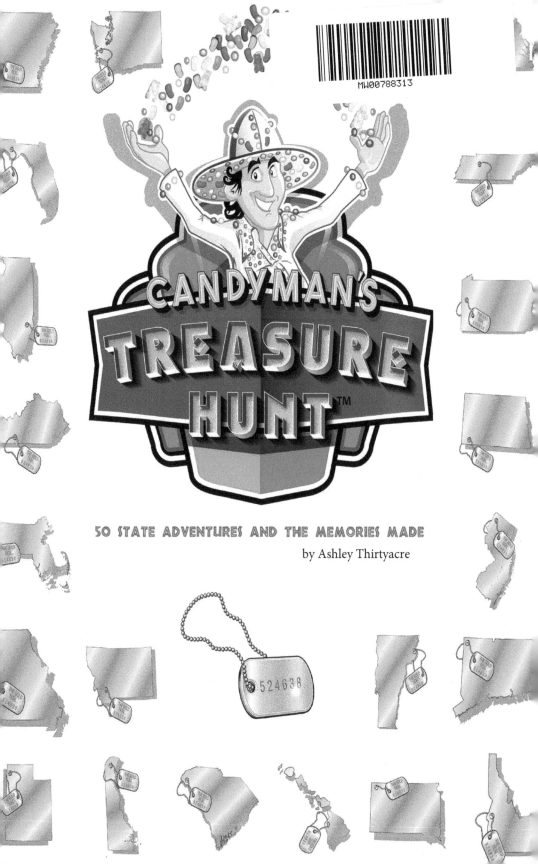

CANDY-MAN'S TREASURE HUNT™

50 STATE ADVENTURES AND THE MEMORIES MADE

by Ashley Thirtyacre

Candyman's Treasure Hunt:

50 State Adventures and the Memories Made

by Ashley Thirtyacre

ISBN: 978-1-7362363-3-8

Table of Contents

50 STATE ADVENTURES AND   THE MEMORIES MADE

DEDICATIONS AND ACKNOWLEGMENTS

We would like to dedicate to all those new Treasure Hunters that have become like a family to us. Many of you have said how we made 2020 a better year for all of you, but you'll never know as there are no words to describe what you all did for us. We are forever grateful to each of you.

We would like to thank a few people who made The Gold Ticket 2020 possible. To Mindy who dropped everything to work 48 hours in a day in those first few weeks to help organize the viral craziness that we were so fortunate to have before us. To Kyle and Kory (The Twins) who learned every aspect of setting up an office to handle a completely different business model from the candy business to treasure hunting. They were able to learn every job needed to make this. To Ernest who threw down his hammer and paint brush to join in anywhere he might be needed. To Tom Kent who jumped in as a volunteer and gave up his ability to search to create a fun atmosphere on our facebook page for people to conversate. To Keith and Ellee who also volunteered and gave up their ability to search in order to help behind the scenes on our facebook page.

David and Stephanie

I'd like to thank David.....for taking someone with agoraphobia and giving me the courage and security to do so many things that I could never have imagined possible. I look at so many situations differently after being schooled by you in everything from A to Z. I appreciate your friendship, your kindness, your creative genius(I get to say that since you're too modest), and your positive spirit. You mean the world to me and so many. To Ashley the author and my daughter who made this book possible with her gifted book making skills and completed it on time. To Ryan my son who cheered us on from across the country.

Stephanie

To Rebecca who has always been there for any crazy idea I came up with and supported me 100%. I'm so happy you were able to see this wonderful treasure hunt before you left on your next journey. I love you and will always miss you.

To Stephanie I want to thank you for opening up an unbelievable world that I never would have had any access to or knowledge about...The treasure hunt community. There were times where frustration could have easily derailed the whole project, but your sense of determination would not let that happen. What's nice is that this is only the beginning.

David

I've known Stephanie and David for several years now, and when she told me about the Gold Ticket, I immediately saw how positively it would affect people's lives, and I wanted to be a part of bringing some happiness and adventure into the world at such an uncertain time in history. At first, I volunteered, then quickly realized just how well I fit into this role, and Stephanie and David did also, because they soon hired me full-time. They are absolutely wonderful to work for and have been extremely generous to me and my family.

This "job" has given me a new purpose and brought a sense of contentment into my life. I love reading the stories from searchers and seeing the pics of families having grand adventures together. I go to bed with a feeling of satisfaction every night that I've helped people in every way I can along the way. I'm looking forward to the 2021 hunts and beyond as we continue to improve and grow. I'm confident that we will continue to bring joy into the lives of thousands of people every year, and that is a wonderful feeling.

FROM TOM

I was so excited to get a ticket to do The Candyman's Gold Ticket Treasure Hunt! As I was waiting for my state, I learned so much about David (The Candyman) and Stephanie while watching their live shows. I was fascinated by his knowledge of candy and the kindness of both of them. Then, I began interacting with all of the awesome group members and having so much fun! Before I knew it, I was doing official games, writing fun riddles, moderating and helping out behind the scenes. I even got to meet the Candyman, who is truly one of a kind! I honestly and truly feel that my experience with this is far more valuable than any prize I could have won. Thank you!

I10 long years to be exact. That's the very first time I ever heard of David Klein aka the Candyman. Came home after working a ten hour shift at the port. I turned on the tv and came across this documentary called the David Klein story. As I was watching this I was very impressed but felt a bit sad in what happened to him. Quote. In life you only have to be a genius for 15 Seconds if you have a idea you can run with this idea this is America. I was so incredibly interested in the way he presented himself and such. Years passed as I always wanted to talk to him. I finally found a phone number for him and I would call

It but I would always hang up, haha. Fast forward to 2020 the year wasn't the greatest I was so depressed and worried about what was going on in the world I about lost it. Sept 7 came and I came across the first time I saw David Klein was having a treasure hunt Aka the gold ticket. I was like omg we gotta play this. I showed my wife and we bought PA and DE. I was so exited. Days passed I watched a few YouTube videos and such so I decided what the heck I'm gonna message David. No answer. I was a bit bummed but figured maybe he was so busy that's why he didn't answer me. So I decided I'm gonna message Stephanie maybe she will answer me. Low and behold a few hours passed and then she answered me and she said to me , "Would you like to talk to David?" I was like, "Um, ok." I was so exited yet it didn't feel real. I was finally gonna talk to the man I've been in awe with for years. He called me and we talked. I was so tongue-tied, lol. I was prolly makin no sense. From that day on we have become friends with David and Stephanie. My wife and I can't thank you enough for letting us play a part in this. Our friendship is far more valuable then any prize. Both of you are truly amazing people. And I thank you for all you have done to help me get outta my darkness to helping our 56k plus members for making their world a better place. We love you guys. And thanks again!

ALABAMA

Winner: Jason Gschwend

Anniston Freedom Riders Mural - Anniston, AL

Oct 21, 2020 at 11:00 am - Oct 21, 2020 at 2:39 pm

Riddle:
Jen wasn't in Virginia when she brought flowers to her Mom
The threshold they were crossing was not very calm paint
showed the history and sound came from near Wish I could
say I'm sorry, even though I wasn't even there.

Alabama
Team Gschwend: Steel Dragon
Team Leader: Jason Gschwend
Team Commander: Don Stallings,
Cash Cab Gypsy Commander: Blake Champion
And there We where....

At a critical juncture south of Birmingham, the Steel Dragon team was cruising when the lifelife engaged and the team began decifering the riddle further.
Jennifer....Jennifer Annistead=Anniston, AL has too be. Yes, mothers day...mother's day burning, threshold to the deep south, memorial, Freedom Riders...UTurn, UTURN!!!

Traveling 1.5 hours to Annisten, AL we arrived with a hunter already in the allyway at 12:15. It would not be until 12:53, Jason was in the Alleyway taking a picture with his phone of a small drain opening under the steel door threshold......Could it be let me see.....yes (bleep, bleep) Yes we (bleepin found it Don!
12:45 the same time in History the Freedom Riders Bus arrived in the Alleyway. Winning 5000.00 and feeling the adenaline rush of joy yet being humble to where We stood was the greatest experience of 2020. Team Gschwend/Steel Dragon Mount Up, it's time to Hunt!

Alabama Memories

"JEN WASN'T IN VIRGINIA WHEN SHE BROUGHT FLOWERS TO HER MOM. THE THRESHOLD THEY WERE CROSSING WAS NT VERY CALM. PAINT HOWED THE HISTORY AND SOUND CAME

ALASKA

Winner: Jennifer Strickland

Rock Man - Anchorage, AK

Oct 23, 2020 at 12:00 pm - Oct 25, 2020 at 12:47 pm

Riddle:
Mr. John met Mr. Stewart at Mr. Tylers
Imagine taking the train downtown and you'll be a
smiler
Go to Philadelphia and do what it takes
To go to the Arctic and buy a Kodiak and Shake!

Clue 1:
Yesterday's riddle was on the radio so loud
I loved it so much my head was in a cloud
With my arms stretched out so wide
A bird landed on them with pride

Clue 2:
If you thought Elton you were on the right track.
The first riddle was all about music, it's fact. What
genre is here and here to stay
Behind the tree and on the ground it lay
P.S. We told Karen where he is.

The Army sent me to Anchorage in '90 and I've been in Alaska ever since. I was kicking myself for not recruiting my friend, Paul (a retired firefighter), and his wife, Karon (a retired flight attendant), sooner. It wasn't until just days before our hunt began that I remembered they craft scavenger hunts for their grandkids. Stumped by the first clue, I invited virtual members Emily (PA), Rebecca (LA), and Shannon (WI) to our team. They left no stone unturned with their dogged research efforts and helped rule out countless hiding places.

We thoroughly enjoyed the hunt and learning SO much about landmarks, parks, statues, and sites we previously knew nothing about here in our very own backyard. The first day, we scoured downtown near the train station, the long staircase (certain the first clue was a "Rocky" reference), the Eisenhower Statehood Monument, and the wooden bear carved statue. Paul and grandson, Finn, searched totem poles, the Parkstrip, and downtown and midtown parks while I checked out what would've been J Street, Earthquake Park, and the Arctic Roadrunner (just two blocks from where the necklace was hidden). Day 2 had us staged downtown when the second clue dropped and soon we raced to the soaring eagle statue in Peratrovich Park (right across from Hard Rock Café) to find many fellow hunters with the same idea. Karon and Paul then headed to Government Hill while I searched the entire grounds of the KBear radio station, the airport and the Aviation Museum. That evening, Rebecca suggested Polar Bear Playground in Russian Jack Springs Park, and it sounded like such a great match, she went with me virtually to explore it at midnight. Not there. Not at the toy plane, airport, polar bear, ravens, the northern lights, nor the skate park next door.

Sunday, Day 3, at Karon and Paul's. The third (and final) clue drops. We all start thinking and talking and I start googling. When I got to the images for "Anchorage railroad rock marker" I see a photo and ask them, "Is there a Rock Man in Anchorage?" And they both know there is and exactly where. Paul leaves to get our coffees and Karon and I race to Alaska Wild Berry. As we near, I'm chanting, "Please, don't let there be headlights! Please, don't let there be headlights!" We pull in front of the building next door and where a car is already parked. But no one is around. When Karon points to the huge Rock Man in answer to my "Where is he?" I'm shocked at his size. We run to it, looking behind it, under the bush. When it hits me that it's a tree we need, we both turn at once to the left and spot the tree. Karon's flashlight comes around and we both simultaneously see the few visible gold-tone beads. Our eyes pop out as we look at one other and quick reach down to turn over the rock – and find the gold ticket underneath! We squeal and scream and hug and laugh and scream some more! What an unbelievable rush!

Alaska Memories

ARIZONA

Winner: Vince Passalacqua

Two Guns Ghost Town Mountain Lions - Winslow, AZ

Dec 5, 2020 at 10:00 am - Dec 5, 2020 at 11:31 am

Riddle:
A couple cats were a sight to see
You gotta leave to be with me
The cornerstone is right there you know
The neighbors have the best art show

To say that I was intrigued from the moment I heard about the Candyman's treasure hunt is an understatement. The story was on all the media outlets and I couldn't help but to imagine how I'd react if I found the coveted prize. Visions of Charlie Bucket's elation as he and his family celebrated his unlikely find raced through my head. Although I didn't know how the hunt was going to work, I figured Iâ€™d take a shot and plunk down my $49.98 with the hopes that the Gold Ticket would be hidden somewhere in Northern Arizona. Then I anxiously waited, and waited for the release of Arizona's riddle.

Nerves turned into stomach butterflies as I struggled to sleep the night before the hunt. The thrill of the chase already had me in its grasp. I woke up early and drank enough coffee to keep someone up for a week. The riddle dropped and I went into panic mode. What does it mean? Which words are important? I had a sick feeling of not knowing where to go, but the rush of knowing that I need to go somewhere, fast.

The first line of the clue mentioned a couple of cats. My mind immediately went to Tucson, as the mascot of the University of AZ is the Wildcats. My heart dropped. There was no way I could drive four hours and be the first one there. Then I thought about mountain lions. These large cats live all over AZ, even the bus system in Flagstaff is called the Mountain Line. I searched the internet for mountain lion statues in AZ. A picture of the rocky ruins of an old roadside attraction at Two Guns, on old Route 66 came up. The old paint on the ruins read, "Mountain Lions", as it had been previously used as a zoo of sorts. The last line of the riddle said that the neighbors have the best art show. I immediately thought of the Painted Desert, which is still miles and miles away from Two Guns, but in the same direction from where I was. I now know that I interpreted that clue incorrectly, but in the moment, it was enough to tell my girlfriend where I was headed, jump in the truck and check it out.

With an eye out for highway patrol, I drove as fast as I safely could. 40 miles passed with a blur as I tried to occupy my mind by poorly singing along to whatever songs were on the radio. I took exit 230, looking for any signs of other vehicles that may have beaten me to the spot. My adrenaline started running as no one else was around. I pulled up to the ruins and almost forgot to put the truck in park before jumping out. I looked around, scanning where the ruins met the ground, looking for the rock from the clue. When I saw the rock, I couldn't believe it. I remember thinking, "There's no way this is really happening." I flipped the rock over and started to brush the dirt away when I revealed part of the chain. There's no way to describe the feelings I experienced in that moment. The elation, disbelief, excitement, happiness, and more disbelief. I pulled the cold necklace out of the ground and held it up, gazing at it in awe. I looked around, still no one. I let out a celebratory howl and realized that I needed to share the moment with those who have supported me and my endeavors. I called my girlfriend, my parents, and my siblings. It was so great to hear their excitement! I hopped back in the truck and drove home at a much more legal speed, smiling all the way.

In my phone interview with the Candyman and Ms. Thirtyacre, I mentioned that I might use the money for an engagement ring for the love of my life. I stayed true to my word and can't wait for what's to come for us. I so greatly appreciate the Candyman for this opportunity and hope he knows what wonderful impacts this nationwide hunt has had on so many people. Thank you to all that helped make this a reality and Mr. Candyman, thank you sir!

Arizona
Memories

ARKANSAS

Winner: LeeAnn Branch

Riverfront Park - Little Rock, AR

Dec 5, 2020 at 1:00 pm - Dec 5, 2020 at 3:35 pm

Riddle:
The way The young one Thought to Play
Was below the bush on this fine day Look
Up and You Can See them rolling you know
Charlie says while looking below

We were so ready for the Arkansas hunt to begin. It was my dad, step mom, and me searching for this treasure. My dad knows Arkansas better than anyone I know and my step mom and I are both good at riddles and full of random facts, so we were sure we could decipher the clues and find the necklace. We decided to grab lunch and be ready to go as soon as we got the clues, so we waited for noon.
It's noon... Here's the Clue!

Oh, what is this?? I am not sure what any of this means or where this is supposed to lead us to. We quickly started running through random possibilities. In the end, all of our theories were wrong, but they still led us to the right place and you'll hear about that below.

Quick, what are the capital letters? Someone on one of the previous puzzles said to look at the capital letters and they may spell something. " TTTPWLUYCSC" Crap. There's only one vowel.   That doesn't spell anything.

Oh! I know it... It's The Old Mill in North Little Rock. The mill has a water wheel that rolls and spins the grist mill. It is in a park where there are a lot of bushes and stones that match the picture. We've got this.
We take off to North Little Rock, about 45 minutes from our home.   When we arrive, we find we are not the only treasure hunters with the same idea. There are five other groups there AND a wedding has just finished up. The happy couple and their wedding party are trying to take pictures. I'm sure there are some terrific pictures of us and other treasure hunters digging in bushes in the background of a lot of their photos. Oops. This is clearly the wrong place, we need to rethink this.

I sat down on a bench and reread the clues. Oh! That's it! It's at the Clinton Library in Little Rock. The young one refers to President Bill Clinton because he was young at the time he became president and he was before (below) or after a bush! There are bridges all over the area which must mean what is rolling above, so we just have to match the rock and bush to the picture (Who the heck is Charlie???)

Thirty minutes later we are at the Library and 15 minutes later we realize nothing else matches up. We are right next to Riverfront park, but that is just too easy, right? We are out of ideas so we might as well go walk around and see if anything matches the picture. There are so many bridges in this area, foot bridges, railroad bridges, and car/truck bridges. Lots of things to look up and see rolling, and there are playgrounds for the young ones. There are lots of treasure hunters at Riverfront Park. A lot have metal detectors, some, like us, are just looking around in the bushes and running around with their phones trying to match a picture to a rock and bush. We had decided it was not at Riverfront Park either and that we needed to leave and regroup and find something to drink.

We went back to the car and drove through the cul-de-sac at the end of the park to get one last look on the way out. As we did, my Dad pointed at a group of bushes that looked slightly different from the rest of the ones in the park. We parked and hopped out and I began to try to match the picture to the rocks. There was a plaque that read "In A Child's Mind" right beside a bush with rocks that lined up. This looks right! I got down and looked and there it was! I couldn't believe that no one had found it before us. There was another group right behind us and someone not involved in the hunt came up and talked to us and asked us about it and said there had been another group looking all over that area, but they had just left. It was sheer luck that we were the ones that found the Treasure and we are very grateful.

Thank you, David and Stephanie, for providing these wonderful experiences for us and everyone across the United States. We have enjoyed keeping up with the other states and seeing all the smiling faces and families getting out and enjoying themselves. You have been a blessing to so many in a rough year.

Arkansas Memories

CALIFORNIA

Winner: Nicole Meneze

Centennial Park - Oroville, CA

Nov 21, 2020 at 11:00 am - Nov 22, 2020 at 12:49 pm

Riddle:
The man was over 80 years old and wore a nifty hat
The lady was 100 and her right tire was flat
A little left and a little down below was the coffee
cup you know
The soggy birds loved the rain dancing on their toes

Clue 1:
The Candyman never liked Buttered Ppcrn jelly
beans
Wet birds don't really fly as they aren't machines
May 30th is my birthday past tense
Dimes, Nichols, Quarters make perfect sense

Our names are Nicholas and Nicole Menezes, or Nick and Nikki for short. We like to say we got married solely for our matching names, as we won't forget them when we get old. We live in the Central Valley of California and have both grown up here for most of our lives.

We purchased tickets for this hunt not knowing what to expect. We are huge travellers and 2020 has definitely halted our travel for the time being, so we jumped on the opportunity to have a little adventure. We honestly did not expect to win, and went into the hunt more for the fun and the experience.

The CA hunt lasted one full day, and a couple hours on day two. On the first day, we seemed to be of the same mindset as many other hunters, finding ourselves in the same area (Auburn) as lots of others. Early the next morning, the words in the riddle clicked for us, and we quickly made our way to, what ended up being, the winning location. Words cannot describe the excitement that we felt when we found the Gold Necklace. Our hearts were racing, we were both screaming in shock, I was crying, and I believe it was one of the most joyful moments in our lives. We will be using the winnings toward our dream of building a mobile coffee business. This was a wonderful experience and we can't thank David and Stephanie enough for creating such a fun adventure during such stressful times.

COLORADO

Winner: Kathy Smith

Castle Rock Park - Castle Rock, CO

Nov 28, 2020 at 1:00 pm - Nov 29, 2020 at 10:58 am

Riddle:
Mark the rich man landed his best job yet
he could see his home from all around so there
was no threat
park your car and out you go
read the words and look by Dennis' toe

When the riddle was released, I knew within an hour where it was hidden. I was convinced that the Gold Ticket was hidden in the small town of Raymer, CO because I had googled famous Marks, and the singer Sugar Ray's real name is Mark. This is a CandyMan hunt, so it had to be related to sugar, right? The next line had the word "see" and I thought the riddle was hinting at "sea." Mer can be translated as sea, so when you put Sugar Ray and sea together, you get Raymer. My husband was looking for any points of interest near Raymer, and the only thing of interest he could find was a picture of a windmill. I was sure Dennis' toe had to be at the foot of a windmill. Windmill, Miller, Dennis Miller... Off we go to Raymer CO, 150 miles from home. When we got to this small town (population 109), we saw a few windmills, but nothing that was on public property. After driving all over this little town multiple times, it suddenly dawned on us that we may have taken the wrong path. We were exhausted at this point and it was getting dark, so we decided to head home. We knew no one else had found the ticket, so the plan was to wait for a new clue that would be announced the next day.

When I woke up Sunday morning, I did another google search of famous Marks. This time I saw that Mark Rosner was a writer for The Rock. I knew Rock Park was in Castle Rock since I had driven past it many times. This time we wanted to make sure we were headed in the right direction before we left the house, so we researched how the name Dennis fit in. I googled Castle Rock and Dennis and found out that there is a character named Dennis in the TV show "Castle Rock." So once again, off we go. As we got closer to Castle Rock it was easy to see how accurate the 2nd line of the riddle was. We could see The Rock from miles away. After parking in the parking lot, we looked around and very quickly saw the exact location that was in the picture attached to the riddle. We began digging... and to our incredible excitement, we found the Gold Ticket!

It was only later when I was talking to Stephanie and David that I realized that the riddle had nothing to do with famous Marks or a character from a TV show. We had found the Gold Ticket based on pure luck and incorrect assumptions. That made me realize how very fortunate we were to be the lucky winners.

My husband and I will always remember how much fun we had together on this adventure, and we will be forever grateful to the CandyMan for generously creating this amazing hunt. From the bottom of our hearts, thank you!!

Colorado Memories

Colorado
Memories

CONNECTICUT

Winner: Seth Mayers

Time Capsule Plaque - Windham, CT

Oct 24, 2020 at 10:00 am - Oct 24, 2020 at 12:39 pm

Riddle:
Blowing pages that do not cost
Look for time that seems so lost In
1944 this really got big and wide In
2013 the kids made this guide

I was reading the news one morning and saw a story about a national golden ticket scavenger hunt. The article wasn't sure it was legit, but I took a shot and bought tickets for Rhode Island, Connecticut and New Hampshire. I gathered my team and we anxiously awaited the hunt. The Rhode Island clue was released and we were convinced that it had to do with Roger Williams. We were unfamiliar with how the clues worked so we assumed that they would revolve around some sort of key figure or landmark in the State. We also assumed that all of the words in the clues would have meaning. We drove up and down the state and poured over Google. We even located a memorial to someone named "Tarzan" and we were convinced we were in the right spot. But alas... We were not. After additional clues came out and the necklace was found, we were left scratching our heads. Even with an explanation we were at a loss as to how anyone could have found the location without dumb luck or the luxury of being intimately familiar with the obscure park in question. I was honestly disheartened with the hunt. So much so that I was tempted to give up on CT and NH. Fortunately the realities of life in the Covid era left me with nothing at all better to do on the next Saturday morning so I kept refreshing my screen anxiously awaiting the CT clue. When it opened up I jumped into it with all of the tips and tricks I'd learned from the RI hunt. The first line referenced "blowing". I immediately thought "Blowing could be wind... wind could be Windsor Locks"... Windsor Locks happened to be a town I was familiar with so it came to mind first. The clue came with a picture of a tree and I had happened to find a website with famous CT trees. (The internet literally was a website for everything). I poured thru the images and didn't find a match. Around that time my girlfriend suggested that "low cost pages" could be a library. Armed with that, I went back to the tree website looking for trees near a library. It was then that I noticed the website had a drop down list for cities. I scrolled to the "W" section and found Windham. The second tree that was listed looked like the picture and was next to the Windham Free Library. Jackpot!!! We literally ran to the car and took off. The GPS said it was only 26 miles away!!

Unfortunately we got stuck behind a trailer hauling horses. It was an agonizing 40 minute drive, but when we finally pulled in, the tree was just as I expected. I sprinted over... dug thru the dirt with my fingers and pulled out the necklace. I was then ridiculous for the rest of the day. I wore the necklace proudly and basically made everyone around me bow down to my Golden Ticket magnificence. We celebrated with a pile of wonderfully cooked filets that would have satiated a hungry caveman. An epic rebound from the RI hunt.

My CT victory gave me confidence to tackle the NH hunt. After several clues (and a brilliant Gorham Silver connection via my girlfriend), I found myself standing in front of a train with a giant 7531 on it. I was convinced I was at the right spot. I spent hours searching that train. Nothing.

After a day of thinking, I was still convinced. So much so that I drove back to the train to await the next clue. Sure enough, it cemented that I was at the correct spot. I spent another hour searching the train. Nada. Sadly two hours later, someone that the very same spot fount the ticket. Hidden INCHES from where I am sure my fingers were. I even took pictures of the spot and submitted them asking if it was possible that it was missing. I could not possibly have gotten any closer without find it. Luckily when I feel the crushing sadness of my near miss, I just put on my necklace and am reminded of my CT glory and all is right with the world.

DELAWARE I

Winner: Gunnar Folke

Pearl Harbor Memorial - Smyrna, DE

Oct 17, 2020 at 1:00 pm - Oct 17, 2020 at 1:41 pm

Riddle:
So The Gold Ticket is not here
may you email me your answer with no fear you
need to find the spot that I am
row over to me faster there is no dam
now tell me what is in front of the flag that you see
at the place you are, 6 letters I need
Email delaware@thegoldticket.com
I will tell the right answer where to find
The gold ticket was previously mine

There was a release of the riddle and we had to submit an answer. I had submitted the answer "anchor" and we had won! We were the first to submit the correct answer. After we had the answer to the riddle, were able to locate the ticket. There was a redo scheduled after this hunt had been completed. This was an awesome experience!

DELAWARE II

Winner: Denny Gyurisin

Augustine Beach - Port Penn, DE

Nov 4, 2020 at 3:00 pm - Nov 5, 2020 at 5:26 pm

Riddle:
Did the hippo cross the street and eat the gourmet food?
In the fall the farm is nice and puts you in a mood
The summer is the best of all, and you must go near there
Find a lonely tree with rocks so you can find it's glare

Clue 1:
The sporty shirt kept wanting to tell us some news
The big huge house is where we can snooze It's old but
two new, let's have some fun
It's cold now, but we love the sun.

My name is Denny Gyurisin and along with my wife Patty and younger son Jayden, we are the lucky finders of the Golden Ticket for Deleware. I am a store manager for Dollar General and my wife is a RN. Jayden is 10 years old and currently in 5th grade. We live in at the Jersey Shore. We love all types of activities like hiking, road tripping, cruising, and enjoying the craft beer scene. Our summers are spent at the beach or our pool and winters dreaming about the upcoming summer.

The Gold Ticket hunt came to us one weekend in August when we were sitting at our pool and my Assistant Store Manager, Kim McFaddon, sent me the link to the article about the hunt. We were immediately intrigued and looked further into it. Within 10 minutes we purchased the NJ hunt. While we were waiting for the NJ date to arrive, we saw that our neighboring state DE, was on a Saturday (NJ was on a Thursday). We thought it would be fun to make a day out of it and do DE as well, so we purchased that state as well. Fast forward to October 29, 2020 and the release of the NJ clue. We centrally located ourselves at a restaurant for lunch for the release of the clue. Once it came out we were dumbfounded and didnt know what direction to head. Needless to say, we were not even close on this one.

On the day of the Delaware release we took the Cape May Lewes Ferry from NJ to DE and had lunch waiting for the clue release. Once it came out we had some ideas and headed in that direction. Within minutes the Gold Ticket was claimed and our adventure was over. Due to this riddle being an "arm chair" clue and not a "boots on the ground" clue, David and Stephanie decided to give DE a redo. Thankfully for us! My wife and I rearranged our work schedule since the clue was released on a Wednesday this time. We headed to DE to await the clue.

Once it came out we had a few ideas and started to head south to the Rehoboth area. We searched that area and some neighboring parks with no luck. It was fun running into other hunters along the way. We searched well into the darkness with no luck. After heading back to NJ, we both had to resume work the following day. While at work we still texted back and forth about possible areas to look as we awaited clue #2. I was talking to my Assistant, Kim (The same one who originally told us about the hunt) and we were dissecting the clue piece by piece. She came up with the idea that St. Augustine of Hippo made a ton of sense which brought us to a park in Northeastern DE.

After pulling up Google Earth and looking at the area, we were pretty sure we were on the right track. Problem was I was at work 2 hours away from the location. My wife could not leave work which left me and my son Jayden. I didnt want to drive all the way to DE again only to be wrong. Plus clue #2 was due to be released in 2 hours. Kim convinced me that I needed to go and practically pushed me out the door. So away I went. I picked up Jayden and headed back to DE. We were less than 10 minutes to the site when the 2nd clue was released. Once I read it, I was convinced we were heading to the right location.

Once there we started our Boots on the Ground search. There was one other hunter there when we arrived. We searched the area for over an hour with no luck. As it started to get dark, we reread all the clues and kept looking. As we were pondering what to do, Jayden picks up a rock and places it near a lone tree. I asked what he was doing and he said he was throwing off any other hunters that may show up. He then said there is one more rock that he wanted to move. Low and behold that was the rock that hid the Gold Ticket! After well over an hour of searching Jayden has found it. So very excited I texted my wife (who thought it was a joke and didnt beleive me) and Kim to let them know we found it. I then0 sent the email to alert David and Stephanie. The drive back to NJ was much more enjoyable this time around.

This hunt was amazing! From the first NJ one to both DE hunts, we had an amazing time. During what happens to be a challenging year, this hunt brought fun and excitement to our lives just when we needed it most. We are so thankful to David and Stephanie and everyone envolved in all aspects of The Gold Ticket. Thank you for shining a bright light into a very dim year!

Delaware II
Memories

FLORIDA

Winner: Justin Simmons Jr.

Apalachee Chief Alligator Memorial - Lake City, FL

Oct 23, 2020 at 11:00 am - Oct 23, 2020 at 1:24 pm

Riddle:
The Alligator went to town, riding on a pony He
didn't like salt one bit at all, on his macaroni
Stare left, and pledge the spot
Woo Hoo you found the necklace worth a lot

My name is Justin Simmons and I found the Florida golden ticket. I live on the east coast of Florida almost 2 hours from the location the gold ticket was hidden. I had been anticipating the hunt for weeks, entertaining the thought of potentially winning the $5k. I would imagine how amazing it would feel but would also tell myself that being 1 out of 1000 hunting parties my odds were pretty low. Still, I scheduled to take part of that Friday off work starting at riddle release at 11 am. I imagined the riddle taking some time to solve and that I would bring my son along for the hunt once he got out of school. Well, the riddle released and within 3 minutes I realized where it had to be. I went with my gut that the yankee doodle lyrics were a red herring and drove to the city formerly known as Alligator town: Lake City. I drove quite fast and made the journey in about 1 hr and 45 minutes. I parked about a block away from the historical marker in downtown Lake City. As I approached and got my bearings for the clue "stare left and pledge the spot" I noticed a few other hunters come walking up. My heart rate increased suddenly and I flew like a flash to the first flag pole I saw. I searched the bushes feverishly as the other hunters did the same. I saw a painted rock and snatched it reflexively. It was unrelated but my mind was in hunt mode. I was having no luck searching through multiple bushes when I looked up and realized; there was another flag pole that was more directly to the left of the historical marker. I hadn't noticed at first as it had no flag. It was at this flag pole that there was a very small bush directly at its base. I knew it had to be this bush. The note with the riddle said to look gently in the bush. I saw nothing. I recalled Florida had just had 2 weeks of torrential rains. I started to look in the dirt and leaves at the bottom middle of the bush. Then I saw the very edge of something that looked like it glinted in the light. My heart stopped in disbelief and I lost my sense of hearing and time for just a moment. I was telling myself that I was about to pick up the gold ticket but I was just wasn't believing it. I picked it up and all my senses came back to me. I called out "I found it" to the other hunters in the area. It was bittersweet as I was so happy to win but I felt bad that others had come so close. We had all known where it was hidden right away and it turned into a race which I happen to win by seconds. Some of the riddles have been mental marathons and some, like mine, were a quick-witted sprint.

I held the gold ticket for days in disbelief that I had actually won. Some days it still feels surreal. I have since been in amazing conversations and friendships with other winners and other hunters who post on Facebook. My son did not get the chance to join me for Florida's hunt but we had a father-son roadtrip to hunt Mississippi which took us to visit with family 400 miles away. I also went to Indiana to hunt with my friend whom I haven't seen in person in 15 years. Thank you Candyman for the memories and excitement. This hunt was was a pebble of happiness tossed into a pond and the ripples are still being seen and felt long after.

Florida Memories

GEORGIA

Winner: James Napier

Welcome Center - Exit 1

Sep 30, 2020 at 11:00 am - Oct 3, 2020 at 3:20 pm

Riddle:
I can I can find this middle first in a place
I can not sale it with an arms race
I do not want to fight as I am a happy space.

Clue 1:
How do you do,
How are you,
Hello

Clue 2:
Between the boards down below you can't see a thing.
Relief is in sight.
The spheres will sure sting.

Clue 3:
I'll sale you a treat
Just mention my name
and you'll get a good seat.

We are the Napier family from Atlanta, Georgia and we are The Gold Ticket finders for Georgia. We set off as soon as we started reading the riddle release. This led us to the Welcome Center off of i75. When we started reading the riddle I knew it had something to do with a cannon, the part where it read "I can I can", and the clues that had the welcomes fit perfectly with the welcome center. We were originally searching the barrel, and then we were at the cannon and the kids were poking around and one of them shouted "We see something shiny!!" and the rest was history. We had so much fun on this adventure! We had originally found out about The Gold Ticket on Facebook and thought this would be a great adventure and fun for the kids. We are so glad we did this and look forward to the future hunts!

50 STATE ADVENTURES AND   THE MEMORIES MADE

HAWAII

Winner: Joseph Kam

Kuhio Beach - Honolulu, HI

Dec 5, 2020 at 3:00 pm - Dec 5, 2020 at 4:10 pm

Riddle:
Feeling bold is where I'll go
You won't feel bored don't you know
It's why you're here that you will see
make a wish and feel glee

My friend Curtis and I(Joseph) teamed up because we've been friends for over 20 years since he was stationed in Hawai'i. I'm a Hawaii resident...born and raised here. We were out at about brainstorming since the early morning before the riddle broke.

When the riddle broke; we were a few miles away...We were actually headed toward Hilton Hawaiian Village on the other side of Waikiki. Looking at the picture it's common foliage all over the island...But, figured the rainbow tower of the Hilton. It was by a hunch that I told Curtis to head toward Waikiki. As we drove to Waikiki...As we approached the beach...We spotted a fountain...I said "let me out" and I crossed the street to the area. About a couple minutes later...A couple of girls came and started looking around...Curtis called and I said "hurry, I'm not alone, I'm not alone...Hurry". In the meantime, the girls and I were leaving no stone unturned. When Curtis arrived...The girls gave up and moved to another spot. Soon after I saw a small rock next to a big rock...I turned in over and dug a little and found the necklace. I gave out a couple yells while jumping up and down that I think pretty much scared some tourists and cops nearby.

Hawaii
Memories

Hawaii Memories

IDAHO

Winner: Angela Barrett

Wallace Living History Museum - Wallace, ID

Nov 7, 2020 at 1:00 pm - Nov 7, 2020 at 2:50 pm

Riddle:
Walk on the sidewalk as the stranger you are
You'll say mine oh mine and not walk too far
I'm yellow and roll as I go to and fro
I'm the power that takes you the way you want to
go

We are so excited to have won this! I was lying in bed thinking of places it could possibly be, when we had read the riddle the museum was still fresh in our minds. My husband, daughter left for the location in the pouring rain. We looked high and low and were able to use the image to find exactly where we thought the gold necklace would be hiding. When we found it, things got very exciting and we were thrilled. This was the most fun we had in all of 2020. We originally had heard about the hunt on Good Morning America and were so glad we chose to be a part of this. We are so looking forward to future hunts and adventures next time. We will be using the money for an apartment, so excited!

ILLINOIS

Winner: Gillian Ziegler

Discovery Depot Train Car - Galesburg, IL

Nov 21, 2020 at 2:00 pm - Nov 21, 2020 at 4:07 pm

Riddle:
He laughed so hard it blew the fort down
Kids art was great to do in town
I was painted green way back in the day
Below the stones you'll find me today

Our team consisted of my husband and I along with our two boys and two golden retrievers. We had deciphered the riddle within about 25 minutes. We knew that "blew" was for Gale and "fort" was burg, and knew our city was Galesburg. I grew up in Galesburg, and we were thinking of other towns that had trains in them. It took about 45 mins for us to drive to the location and find the ticket. We had originally learned about The Gold Ticket treasure hunt on Facebook and purchased our ticket right away. We had so much fun! We are really looking forward to the next hunt!

INDIANA

Winner: Sara Shields

Calumet Trailhead - Chesterton, IN

Nov 14, 2020 at 12:00 pm - Nov 15, 2020 at 10:37 am

Riddle:
I sang while I drifted into the dust
I rode my bike, so I wouldn't rust
I fell from a plane with 6 fine others
It's the RIGHT time for peace don't smoke my brothers

My name is Sara Shields and I found the Gold Ticket in Indiana. I live in Southwest Michigan but given Indiana is 40 minutes away, I am familiar with the northern part of the state. My tale is one of luck and timing," as much as it is about skill. What I won through the hunt is more than money. I also found people I can call friends. My team consisted of my husband and my virtual teammate Amanda Ruffin. It was chance that Amanda and I met online and we are going into our 3rd hunt together.

The Indiana hunt started and it was a beautiful sunny Saturday afternoon. We were in Northern Indiana ready to go. Our initial analysis put us headed south, towards Wilbur Wright and also towards Mitchell, Indiana because of Gus Grissom, part of the Friendship 7. Also, Right Stuff. We had a lovely tour of the area seeing his boyhood home and the rocket monument. Grissom Air Force based was named for Gus Grissom. A true hero, but not the key to the ticket so we headed back north, stopping a few places. We decided to get "unstuck" and start picking the riddle apart from scratch on the car ride while Amanda at home in Ohio worked the clue too. We got home after midnight and I started to catch up on messages. Amanda made the Calumet connection to the peace pipe and connected it to a few locations, including the bike trail but still liked some other areas in Northern Indiana like the Community Veteran's Memorial. At 1:22am, I connected the seven lives lost in Chesterton, IN in 1933. I had not connected the street name of Broadway. I found the trail map prior to sleeping, reviewed it but didn't even see the street names as they moved off the screen when I enlarged the picture. To me, the drifts and dust were the dunes.

On Sunday morning, I left early and alone. Perhaps checking out Mt Baldy first was a bad idea as that was just for pleasure! I started at the trail head of the Calumet Trail, swing and miss. My next stop was the Beverly Shores Train Station parking lot where I inspected the western Calumet trail head- it was prominent, landscaped and the sign was right but no, not the right mulch. I went back to my car prepared to hit the next western trail stop since the sign was accurate to the picture. I was in my car and my back up camera picked up the corner of the east bound trail head. The eastern trail head was back in the corner and not easy to see. In fact, others had been there and not seen it. I exit my car and with my little trowel, I uncovered the Gold Ticket. It was a rush- so hard to explain the adrenaline rush. I was shaking when I messaged Amanda and shared the news!

While on the phone with Stephanie and David, a car pulled up and I got to meet Jason Gschwend, the Alabama winner. As I mentioned above, my tale is one of not just skill but also luck and timing. Enter Jason. That tag was almost Jason's that day but it wasn't meant to be – that right trail was hidden in a corner. What I got from Jason in that parking lot was his congratulations, his enthusiasm, his grace and his authentic kind nature. I am fortunate to have met Jason, Amanda and many others through this amazing experience. Thank you to David and Stephanie for this experience. It is hard to put into words what it means. This year has been very hard and sometimes dark. I lost my mother July 27 and five days later my husband lost his father. In a dark time, this experience brought hope, connection and joy and given me experiences I would have never had otherwise. In a word: priceless.

INDIANA
Memories

IOWA

Riddle:
No one would go with me, sad because the view You
were never second, the first time I saw you You told
me what you were, and how we came to be I'm so
lucky I found it beneath this growing tree

Clue 1:
The guys announced it loud and clear
the dust didn't get in their ears
I counted 244 gone by, oh my!
I was all alone with John and I

Hello everyone! My name is Jonna. I was fortunate enough to discover the Gold Ticket in Iowa. Im excited to share our adventure with you.

The first day the riddle was released I spent hours on the computer searching for town names that resembeled "lonely" or "alone". My partner Katie and I made a 40 minute drive to a small town named Colo (because it rhymed with "solo"). We experienced a rollercoaster of emotions as we ran to a small tree and discovered none other than a golden discarded candy wrapper. Defeated and befuddled with the riddle we headed back home for the evening to wait (and hope) for the second riddle to be released the following day.

The morning of the second day my friend, Justin, and I drove through a number of towns without any certainty in any of them. We drove around What Cheer (because its a fun town name, had a freedom rock, and 1st and 2nd St), and Lone Tree ("all by myself" part of the riddle). We even drove through Frytown because one of the riddle lines was a direct quote from a book written by James Frey (we were grasping at straws by this point). Due to other circumstances, when the second riddle was released midday, we had only 4 hours to search and were only able to travel about an hour in any direction from Iowa City. At first, some items in the second riddle led us to believe the Gold Ticket was somewhere in Iowa City . In the riddle "244", exit 244 is Dubuque St (1st city in Iowa) which runs through Iowa City. In addition Iowa City is in Johnson County ("John and I"). While Justin and I were searching around Iowa City, two of my team members called me. "Jonna, we feel REALLY strongly that you and Justin need to go to Independence right now!" was the first thing I heard when I answered the phone. My team had found a Liberty Park in Independence that had an official copy of the Declaration of Independence in it! It all fit, Independence ("all by myself", and "alone"), "244 gone by" year 2020 - 244 = 1776 the year the Declaration was signed. John Hancock signed it "John and I" and the park was on 1st St and 2nd Ave. Fortunately, Independence was only 1 hour away from Iowa City. That was the longest 1 hour drive of my life! Justin was driving and I was texting my team with updates as to how close we were. When we pulled up, no one was at the little park. I got so excited I jumped out of the car, ran to the tree from the picture and started digging with my hands. Justin (a bit more collected at this point) grabbed the shovel out of the bag. He started digging and while asking repeatedly "what does it look like?" as I shouted helpfully "its the Gold Ticket! Its the Gold Ticket!". We found the Gold Ticket necklace a few inches down in the dirt next to the tree.

This was such an amazing, exciting adventure. I'd like to thank David and Stephanie for all the hard work and effort they put into this nationwide treasure hunt.

IOWA
Memories

KANSAS

Winner: Lindsay Bunyak

Buffalo Bill Cultural Center - Oakley, KS

Nov 21, 2020 at 1:00 pm - Nov 21, 2020 at 2:05 pm

Riddle:
Oh shoot those specs are fine
I listen to the heavy metal all the time
A horse for a dollar I'd pay
I ate three while the legend runs a stray.

The Bunyak family set out extra early on Saturday, Nov. 21st thinking it would be a weekend road trip in Kansas. We filled the car with snacks, sleeping bags and extra clothes in case we needed to sleep in our car. As we drove into Kansas from Colorado we started to make notes on all of the things we saw along the road. Our first stop happened to be in Oakley, KS. We filled the gas tank and continued on to Wakeeney for some lunch and to await the clue:

1) Oh shoot those specs are fine- Our first thought was glasses - "we just stopped in Oakley those are a type of sunglasses"

2) I listen to the heavy metal all the time- "I wonder if that Buffalo Bill statue was metal? Or maybe the train tracks next to it?"

3) A horse for a dollar I'd pay- " Yep Buffalo Bill...dollar bill and he's on a horse!"

4) I ate three while the legend runs a stray- this one was solved by Grandpa- I-83 is the highway that Oakley is on!

As soon as we arrived to the spot we jumped out of the car and raced to the statue. There was one other family that was looking around. We got lucky we happed to look in the correct spot and pull the golden necklace from under the gravel before they did. Next thing you know we were receiving a phone call from David and Stephanie! This was one of the most exciting opportunities we have ever received! It's a day we will never forget!

Thank you from the bottom of our hearts,

Jared, Lindsay, Jackson (13 years old), Eliot (10 years old)

Kansas Memories

KENTUCKY

Winner: Alexander Tracewell

Central Park - Ashland, KY

Oct 16, 2020 at 11:00 am - Oct 16, 2020 at 12:11 pm

Riddle:
I was living in my own Pokemon land.
Eating some coconut chocolate bars and feeling grand
He couldn't stop chatting about how he loved Christmas time
The kids were all playing not far from the pine
Look under look over, it's a rock you want to see
A path is nearby take video for me

We pulled into the parking lot after getting a call from David Klein as soon as we had found The Gold Ticket. We live in Parkersburg, WV and were about 2 hours from Ashland where we had found the Gold Ticket necklace. The first part of the riddle about Pokémon and land we were able to put together the trainer Ash and land. The second part of the riddle about the coconut candy bars and feeling grand we were able to get mounds. We had searched about parks in Ashland with mounds and found Central Park. When we got there and located the mound, we saw the playground and knew we were in the right spot. This was unlike any other experience I have ever had, it was so much fun! There were about 4 other groups at the park searching when we were there, we could tell they were having fun searching as well.

LOUISIANA

Winner: Rachel Voitier

Grand Cote National Wildlife Refuge Sign - Marksville, LA

Dec 12, 2020 at 12:00 pm - Dec 13, 2020 at 9:03 am

Riddle:
David was just 3 years old when he was on his way
He didn't know Flint but met him one day
Magnificent as her mom can know to sew
That doll sure loved to wear a rainbow

I don't believe in coincidences. My husband David first told me about The Gold Ticket hunt after he'd read an article about the Candyman. We have three children, Andrew, Virginia and Lily, so $50 for a weekend's worth of family fun sounded like a bargain. And who knew, maybe we'd even find the Gold Ticket.

When we first read our riddle, our thoughts lead us to look at St. Joseph, Louisiana, since Joseph in the Old Testament wore a coat of many colors. But we couldn't find a spot that warranted getting in the car to look there. We tried again. Was "Magnificent" referring to Morgus the Magnificent of New Orleans fame? Did the "3" in the first line and "one" in the second refer to LA 31? Could we find an intersection that would let "David" and "Flint" meet?

We had read the tribute David had written for his late wife Rebecca. Since Rebecca sewed quilts, maybe "her mom can know to sew" referred to their daughter Roxanne? Virginia researched that there is a Roxy's Diner at a casino in Marksville in Avoyelles Parish. When we learned Avoyel means "Flint people", our family of five jumped in the car for the 1.5 hour drive there! It would turn out that none of those connections were what the clues intended, but no coincidences for us. As we drove backroads into Marksville, we passed a sign for Little California Road and knew we had to be on the right track! Outside the Paragon Casino where Roxy's Diner is located, we looked for a spot that matched our clue photo—nothing. After dinner at a local spot we started the trip home intending to drive down Little California Road. But it was dark and the road was gravel so we decided to just head home and get an early start the next day.

Once home, I pulled up the map and saw Little California Road went right through Grand Cote Wildlife Refuge! I tried street view, moving like the Candyman had as a child, from East to West. When I showed Virginia the Grand Cote sign, she thought we should leave right then at 1:30 am! The next morning, four of us set out again in the dark. The sun rose and the drive was beautiful with clear skies and fall color. As we pulled up to Grand Cote, we could just see a rock under the sign! Virginia and I jumped out of the car, I grabbed the rock and scraped the ground underneath—gold gleamed in the morning sunshine! We had found The Gold Ticket!

Louisiana Memories

MAINE

Winner: Andrew Lindberg

"The World's Largest Telephone" - Bryant Pond, ME

Oct 17, 2020 at 11:00 am - Oct 17, 2020 at 12:51 pm

Riddle:
He ain't swimming over there
A witty man who would be right here
5" deep in back it has sank
We'll show you a picture it is no prank

We pulled into the parking lot after getting a call from David Klein as soon as we had found The Gold Ticket. We live in Parkersburg, WV and were about 2 hours from Ashland where we had found the Gold Ticket necklace. The first part of the riddle about Pokémon and land we were able to put together the trainer Ash and land. The second part of the riddle about the coconut candy bars and feeling grand we were able to get mounds. We had searched about parks in Ashland with mounds and found Central Park. When we got there and located the mound, we saw the playground and knew we were in the right spot. This was unlike any other experience I have ever had, it was so much fun! There were about 4 other groups at the park searching when we were there, we could tell they were having fun searching as well.

MARYLAND

Riddle:
Shoeless Joe Jackson wouldn't play here
He'd be in the Midwest oh my dear
Go over to the boulder by the sign
Dig 4" down and you are fine!

We are the Santiago Velez Team

Ricardo (dad), Victoria (12yo) and Loy (mom). We got excited as soon as we heard that there was a real live treasure hunt for a candy factory.

I want to tell you a little bit of our process. We registered as soon as we found out on September 9. We were soooo excited. We have been planning for this day since day 1. We followed the youtube channel, saw the videos, joined the Facebook page, research places around and follow the scavenger hunts happening in other states. We gave this our 100%, not thinking about the prize but about the journey. We were thrilled to be a part of this wonderful adventure and we are so glad we did it, even if we didn't find the ticket.

On day 1, my husband had to go to work, so he couldn't join us in the hunt, but my daughter and I had our bags made since the day before. Including gardening tools, a flashlight and anything else we thought we might need. We woke up early, had breakfast and sat on our car at 8:30am waiting for the moment the clue was released. We probably refreshed the website 100 times. When we saw the clue, our first hunch was a white water rafting area with the word deer in the name and near some falls. We made 3 stops.

Our first stop was at Deer Creek in White Hall MD (1 hour and 14 minutes away from us.) As soon as we made it there, we knew we got it wrong. There were a lot of private farms so we head out to our second location.

Our second stop was in Deer Creek Picnic Area, (58 minutes from our previous location). We did a quick rest stop but we quickly realized that we were not in the right spot.

Our third stop was in Deer Creek State Park in Forest Hills MD (20minutes from our previous location). We were certain this was the spot. It was a beautiful creek and a wonderful hike. We walked for about 3.5 hours and had no cell signal, at that point, we thought someone might had already found it and had no way to find out. We decided to take the rest of the time to explore and enjoy our hike. We discover many natural treasures and had a blast.

We got home, regrouped and went to bed early to be ready for our next hunt. We were so excited that we couldn't even sleep! We started researching possibilities... finally at 3am we went to bed.

We had a gut feeling that it was going to be closer to Baltimore. We got some breakfast and once again, waited in the car for the clue, refreshing the website every couple of seconds. As soon as the clue hit our brains light up. We know the key was with Shoeless Joe, we searched online and red his story and immediately thought it had to be at a place called/or related to the Black Socks. We searched for baseball fields with the name and immediately head there.

As soon as we got there, there was another pair of treasure hunters looking around. They took a different direction, and my daughter saw the rock and jumped out of the car, gardening tools in hand, and started digging! At that point, in our hearts we knew the tickets was ours to find. As soon as they saw us digging, they started looking around the rock...Finally, a bright golden chain,...we had it! We felt bad for the other hunters but we were rejoiced. We could even believe it! We left a dollar with a note, "we found it!", for anyone else that figured it out. We left, and I immediately sent the email.

It was a great day!

This was wonderful! The journey was amazing and we got so much from this. Our family needed this and it was something we will never forget. If we have learned anything is that life is unpredictable and uncertain and family is everything. Our family had a great day today.

That night, we celebrated with a family meal and a movie night, Willie Wonka and the Chocolate Factory, of course. We thank God for the opportunity, for getting us to our destination safely and enlightening our journey. And we wanted to say thank you David and Stephanie, you are conductors of joy, hope and light during these difficult times. You have made great days for many families and reminded us of that sense of wonder. Pray for you, for many years of health so you can continue making people happy for many years to come.

People like David and Stephanie make the world colorful, brighter, full of swirls and hope, with sprinkles, sparkles, glitter and a cherry on top.

We are living in difficult times, we needed this and we are grateful to the Candy Man for coming up with this wonderful, marvelous and once in a lifetime idea. David Klein is a true creator of wonders. Thank you!

Maryland Memories

MASSACHUSETTS

Winner: Leigh Lessard

Heritage Park - East Longmeadow, MA

Nov 14, 2020 at 10:00 am - Nov 15, 2020 at 12:58 pm

Riddle:
You might one day own this place you search
I don't think you're looking in a birch
First mow the hay it will take you all day
Owl says it's near 2 rocks, he won't lead you astray

Clue 1:
There's no owl here, but his home might be
We aren't in a cemetery as you can see
A compass can get you closer if you ask me
It's TIME to go look in a tree

We are a family of treasure hunters and love the adventure that comes with the hunt. We are two sisters and a brother who work together along with our spouses and kids. Our love of treasure hunting began about 8 years ago when a local jewelry store started hosting annual treasure hunts. The prizes were diamond jewelry and the hunt clues contained riddles and puzzles that took us throughout Connecticut. We won several of the hunts and we were immediately hooked! We later heard of Forrest Fenn's treasure, so we bought the book and even traveled to Montana and Wyoming in pursuit of the treasure. We would have regular family meetings to brainstorm ideas as we worked best as a team. We've worked on a handful of other treasure hunts, like Fandango, Trove, and a few others. When we heard about The Gold Ticket hunts, we knew immediately that we were in!

The MA Hunt started on a Saturday morning. Some of us were at home ready to do research, and others were strategically located at the MA border waiting for the riddle to be released. The clue referenced "mow the hay...all day", and one of us immediately thought of Longmeadow. so we started researching places in that area. We searched many local parks, and we knew we were close because of all the other searchers that we ran into. The clue noted that you could own the place you search someday, so Bliss Park and Heritage Park were our favorites. At the time, we were not thinking that it would be found in a tree because the clue indicated that it was covered by an inch of dirt; we assumed that meant it was buried in the ground.

The next day, we received the hint. Again, we were strategically located in areas that we thought were the most promising. The hint referenced a compass, so we thought that meant it was in East Longmeadow. We had almost given up for the day when one of us discovered that there was a time capsule located in Heritage Park, and the hint mentioned "TIME". We decided it was worth another look, and parked right next to the time capsule and large stone sign for the park. Located next to the time capsules was a tree with a small hole/knot about 4 feet off of the ground. As one of us walked past the tree, something like "you could get an inch of dirt in there!" was said in a joking manner. The other searcher in that car started poking around in the knot, and soon pulled out the Gold Ticket!

While many people we know consider us lucky, we like to attribute our success to hard work and perseverance. In fact, this was our third attempt at winning a Gold Ticket! We had previously tried our home state of Connecticut and Rhode Island, but we weren't fast enough! We love treasure hunting so much that we have even started Northeast Treasure Hunts and hope to get going with our own treasure hunts soon! We would encourage anyone to get involved in this great activity. It is a wonderful time to spend time with family, get outside, and discover amazing new places!

Thank you again, David and Stephanie, for this wonderful opportunity!

Leigh, Katie, Andy and our Families

MICHIGAN

Winner: Catherine Pyle

Rieger Park - Albion, MI

Oct 24, 2020 at 3:00 pm - Oct 25, 2020 at 12:11 pm

Riddle:
The gray heron knew where to go
a pie plate he loved to throw
He loved to eat with a fork
put a line in with a cork
Have fun and enjoy the dough

Dear David & Stephanie,

I first want to say thank you so much for putting this hunt together. My family and I had a lot of fun doing this. Now that we won the money, we can't thank you enough for being so generous. The thrill of winning a Gold Ticket was priceless for us and something we will never forget. When we spoke with you guys on the Live YouTube, to say that we were shocked would be an understatement, I wish I would have been able to gather my thoughts a little better than I did, I was exhausted and so frazzled. I head up a few groups of various things and speaking under stress isn't usually too challenging for me, but I somehow found myself looking at my husband with question on what to say to each question. We found ourselves looking at each other every now and then for the rest of the day laughing and saying "I can't believe it". My husband and I both have "Do-er" Personalities, we both have always worked extremely hard at whatever we do.

So, when we have had down time, that is exactly what we do, nothing, and try to take a break for a moment. I love games and puzzles and riddles so if you give me a task to do or figure out, I'm on it, 200%, I don't give up easily. As my daughter has gotten older, we have forced ourselves to go find adventure in our "down times" for her sake. We found that she is a metal chaser after she did her first kid's St. Patrick's race when she was 6, and so even though I am not a runner and in fact hate running we became monthly 5K runners chasing the pretty medals at the finish lines, and I mean monthly, hot August and freezing January. We have begun to try all sorts of new things that we never would have before. My husband does not like long drives so when I bought this ticket, I approached him gently and didn't tell him my excited thoughts of "Yay, we are going to be driving endless hours in the car and by the way I packed overnight bags."

So, with that said, we have a few places that we frequent in our state, but we don't know it well. We rarely go West at all and had never been to Albion or even heard of the city. It was beautiful. They have done an amazing job on their city parks. It's worth a day trip to those in lower Michigan. I initially wanted to post a pic on the Facebook group of us finding the spot and gold ticket, but after seeing so much negativity regarding Michigan, I decided I didn't want to throw myself into the Lion's Den. Maybe it was luck, that this was just the next best guess for me, but I do feel like Riddles are meant to be challenging. In any riddle that I have ever tried to solve the line has never meant exactly what it is saying, you are looking for anything and everything and sometimes overthinking them. I saw a lot of posts of people saying I just got lucky and recognized the picture, I am not sure anyone that even passed by there every day would recognize that picture.

And now knowing all the details, I still cannot find a picture anywhere online of that plaque memorial. I also don't think anyone would wait 21 hours if they knew where $5,000 was. I am not a person that gets overly excited, I mean I could win the world and you might think I was just awarded a single penny. This was different, unlike my usual self, I was so extremely excited to find this location, that my husband ended up capturing my reaction on video while I was indeed filling the hole back in with its original dirt. I was a little bummed out that someone posted a pic of the site the next day with someone commenting that we didn't fill in the hole, because that's just not who I am. I am not sure if someone thought maybe there was a backup necklace still in there or what, no big deal, we just laughed about it. I don't feel like I owe anyone an explanation, but I just had it on my shoulders to give some clarity into my process and especially after there was so much negativity towards you guys that the riddle didn't make sense or wasn't fair. It was a riddle/puzzle not a race and I know it has taken you so many hours to put all of this together, I am sure it has not been an easy process.

You guys have done an amazing job, Go team David & Stephanie. I hope you have truly enjoyed putting this hunt together. I have really enjoyed reading the stories and posts from people on how it got their families together or out of the house for the weekend or just something to look forward to during this wacky year of 2020. You guys did that, good for you, take that credit. Now, we can't wait for the next big race. So again, we just thank you so much from the bottom of our hearts.

Sincerely,
Catherine

Michigan Memories

MINNESOTA

Winner: Heather Lynn

Battle of Birch Coulee Marker Monument - Morton, MN

Oct 17, 2020 at 2:00 pm - Oct 17, 2020 at 8:12 pm

Riddle:
At 20 he hit his prime, but one not ready to fight
Eight in the morning you come across this blaze of a site
Six men plus were not in lava where you're standing
Come to this strip by trees on road that is banding

CANDYMAN'S TREASURE HUNT

We are Team Lynn- Heather the driver, Zoe the brains and Miley the finder. We found the gold ticket in MN.

Our riddle was released October 17th at 1pm. We planned on going to the laundromat at 11 so we could be done by 1. We failed and got to the laundromat at 1. We had it figured out in 10 mins. We were only 2 and half hours away but we had to wait for the laundry to finish. One of the washers broke on us so we went hunting with wet laundry in the back and we forgot the McGuyver bag we packed for hunting. It was an all or nothing mission as we would have to head home after because we forgot to feed the cats. We were a wreck lol.

The riddle was

At 20 he hit his prime, but one not ready to fight
Eight in the morning you come across this blaze of a sight
Six men plus were not in lava where you're standing
Come to this strip by trees on road that is banding

We figured it out to be the Battle of Birch Coulee in Morton, MN.

Major Joseph R Brown was in his 20's and brought 160+ troops to bury remains of settlers. They were surrounded by 200 Dakota soldiers in the middle of the night and attacked in the morning. We couldn't figure the prime part out but he was in his 20's and they were not ready to fight.

I figured the Eight in the morning meant that it was in the 8 o'clock position if you put a clock on MN it pointed to the spot.

We googled the images before going and there was a picture of foot prints. I thought there would be 6 foot prints. Zoe was researching rocks and lava and found Morton Gneiss began as granite a type of lava 3.5 billion years ago.

Morton Gneiss has banding in it. When we got to the location there was a row of trees and rock. We did not get a lot of time to explore as we had a long drive home. The drive there was tons of corn fields. It was super cold and windy. We plan on going back when its warmer and greener to explore more. We did not see any other hunters and we were the first ones there. A lot of the hunters went to the north shore. We would have too if we didn't think the 8 meant the direction.

This has meant so much to us. I am a single mom raising my girls. I started 2020 with breast cancer. Luckily they were able to remove it all. Being high risk in Covid season working is a challenge and money was super tight. I was so excited to see The Gold Ticket from the Candyman. I did not think we would find it but I really wanted my kids to be able to look back at 2020 and remember the hunt. Not the cancer, covid, online schooling, the riots and the politics. We were able to split some of the money for fun spending, car repairs and paid our rent for the remainder of the year so we could enjoy the holidays a little more.

Thank you so much for this adventure. Can't wait for more.

Minnesota Memories

MISSISSIPPI

Winner: Lisa Rollins

Ivis Tribute Statue Park (The Alzheimer's Tree) - Tupelo, MS

Dec 5, 2020 at 12:00 pm - Dec 5, 2020 at 1:55 pm

Riddle:
I never felt cheated from the man with the shoes
I forgot his name, but he was in the news
I got chills, they're multiplying
Be careful it could be electrifying.

We live in and bought for Mississippi.

The moment I read outlook about the contest my son Evan (10) said "We HAVE to do that!" Daughter Vivien (5) was all in. My husband Matt and I were ready for adventure but the kids just wanted to candy factory!

On the day of the hunt we had bags packed and were heading for an expedition. We could not believe the clue was pointing to our own town!

Although we didn't understand every clue, we drove around to some hunches while we figured out the rest. On our second stop I was walking around a sculpture and saw the Alzheimers plaque. I screamed to my family across the park and starting digging. I dug about 8 ft, bare handed and busting knuckles along the way until the necklace appeared. Screams, high fives and hugs ensued!.

The prize money is great....but those smiles on my children's faces were worth Millions. They each took turns wearing the necklace to school before it found a permanent home on our Christmas Tree.

Love living life's adventures,
Lisa

MISSOURI

Winner: Beka Simmons

Sun Ridge Park - Hillsboro, MO

Nov 28, 2020 at 2:00 pm - Nov 28, 2020 at 4:11 pm

Riddle:
I looked to see what was the time
I knew it would be fun, but I couldn't climb
Thomas didn't lie when he wrote the letter
His son was no everest or anything better

We had so much fun! Definitely the highlight for the year. Mel and I work together, we tattoo in St. Charles, MO. I entered the contest, I'm 100% a dreamer. Mel was the brains that lead us to the spot. We were trying to crack the code at the shop and I was just ready to get on the road before we had it solved. So we picked the county we felt it was in: Jefferson County. Mel searched the history while we were on our way. She found the watch tower so we agreed to try there first. I grabbed the pic of the location it was buried and seen cracks in the cement that was in the photo and a leaf in the same spot in the photo and started digging like my life depended on it! When we found it we screamed and hugged rolled in the dirt, it was awesome!

MONTANA

Winner: Allisa Frese

"Welcome to Laurel" train - Laurel, MT

Nov 7, 2020 at 12:00 pm - Nov 9, 2020 at 10:44 am

Riddle:
On my honor I will find this gold ticket now I promise
Orange you glad you don't need to share it with Thomas
Look under me and find my hiding spot
I'm not on the ground and that says a lot

When I bought my ticket for my great state of Montana, my husband told me I just wasted $50. He didn't think it was legit. I thought it sounded so fun that it was worth a shot. I talked about it for 2 months and convinced him to get on board.

Our team consisted of myself, my husband Jeremy, and our sons Jaylen (19) and Brayde (16). We started doing geocaching to "pregame." We aren't very good at it so we were a little concerned about the state hunt. But I kept saying we were going to win, I just knew it in my soul. I made us all shirts and even one for our dog. We decided on the team name, "Team Snak Pak."

We live in Hamilton, Montana. We decided to drive to Missoula which is 60 miles from our house. We wanted to be there by the time the clue was released so we were better located to jump on the interstate. Our clue was released at 10am and by 10:03 we were driving as fast as we could to Helena, Mt. We were sure it was the place, every clue fit exactly. When we got there, we searched and searched. We didn't find the gold ticket but we did end up at the election protest at the state capitol building, and joined in.

This isn't the place for politics, so I'll just say that our family is passionate about politics and we felt like God put us there to participate. After we marched, we went back to searching. We decided to get a hotel room as we were 3 hours from home and we still felt like it was in Helena. The next day when the clue was released, we still felt as though it was in Helena. We found multiple spots that fit exactly. We went inside of statutes and displays and I stuck my hands in some seriously sketchy dark holes, no ticket! We decided to stay in a hotel again because we figured if it wasn't in Helena, we were still more centrally located than we would be at home. We found the most amazing Chinese food and enjoyed our night just hanging together. At 2 am, I woke up and sat straight up in bed, somehow it came to me in my sleep.

I woke up my husband, I yelled "Laurel, it's in Laurel...Laurel and Hardy, it's there!!" We talked and since we were in the middle of a Blizzard, we decided not go unless we could identify the exact spot as Laurel was 215 miles away. My husband stayed awake for an hour looking for anything train related in Laurel, he found nothing and went back to sleep. Just a few mins after Jeremy went back to sleep at 3 am, I woke up.

I grabbed my phone, googled and the picture popped right up. I started yelling and jumping up and down. Jeremy thought I was nuts, but I showed him the picture and he jumped right up and said, "let's go!" I woke up the boys and we had the hotel packed up, packed in the car and we were on the road in 15 mins. It took us 5+ hours to drive 215 miles because of the Blizzard and the worst road conditions we have ever seen.

We drove 40 mph the entire way on the interstate. We saw 5-10 cars and trucks that had slid off the road. We arrived at our destination just after 8 am. I was jumping out of my seat with excitement. We were the only ones there. There was one set of tracks in the snow and they didn't go under the train, so I knew the gold ticket was still there. We all started looking. I made my way around the train to where my kids and husband had already looked. I repeated a phrase I use often and they hate, "we don't know where it isn't until we know where it is!" I got eye rolls and I think a "ya, ok mom." I went under the train and saw what looked like a tiny piece of dead grass in a very small crack.

I started trying to pull it out with my finger nails and then it popped out! It was the golden ticket!!! I started screaming at the top of my lungs, once again my kids and hubby thought I was crazy and was joking. And then I whipped out the gold ticked and showed them. We all jumped around while yelling in excitement. Once the excitement settled a tiny bit, we realized it was freezing (single digit temps), and we were 8 hours from home. So we jumped in the car and headed home.

 One the way we got the phone call from the Candyman and Stephanie. What a treat that was!! They are celebrities to us. We stopped and got another hotel room about 4 hours from home and again enjoyed the excitement high and just being together. We are so grateful for the entire experience! We are already planning for the "Big Hunt", and I plan on winning that too!

Montana
Memories

Nebraska

Winner: Emilia Brandt

Stockville Historical Marker-Curtis, NE

Nov 14, 2020 at 1:00 pm - Nov 16, 2020 at 5:38 pm

Riddle:
The Great Bambino hit a home run
The Boone's loved to watch him for fun
The Dow Farm was a strange place to wow
I pulled over on the side of the road so I
wouldn't hit a cow

Clue 1:
Did you enjoy the candy in my riddle
I'm now an adult and no longer little
Below the old sharpie you will see
Near the concrete is where I'll be

Clue 2:
Near some trees on the open highway
You'll find my story any time of day
I'm in a fake rock under a dusting of dirt
I drove almost to Tickertown wearing a skirt

My name is Emelia Brandt, and I live in Kearney, NE with my husband and our three children, ages 10, 6 and 3. We really enjoy activities such as geocaching, escape rooms, scavenger hunts, etc., so when I learned about The Gold Ticket on facebook, I decided to sign up.

We received the first riddle on Saturday, November 14 at 12:00 p.m. My husband and I started working to figure out the riddle. We knew, from The Gold Ticket facebook page, that previous riddles were difficult to figure out and often included multiple levels of wordplay. With that in mind, we began researching Babe Ruth, as we knew "The Great Bambino" was one of his nicknames. Within a couple of hours, we came up with two ideas we wanted to pursue. Our research on Babe Ruth had led us to Baby Ruth candy bars, which were originally produced by the Curtiss Candy Company. I knew there was a town in Nebraska named Curtis, and I thought the candy connection might be fitting for this contest. Our other idea was a town named Beaver City, NE. Another nickname for Babe Ruth was "The Behemoth of Bust." Our research told us that Beaver City, NE was the home of the world's largest baby in the late 1800s and that the little girl was nicknamed the "Behemoth Baby."

We loaded up our van and headed southwest toward Curtis at around 2:00 p.m. We arrived around 3:30 p.m. and began searching the baseball field. We thought there might be something to the baseball reference in the riddle, and the baseball field in Curtis happened to have lots and lots of cement steps built into the hillside that resembled the photo we had received. It was also located next to a corral or arena, which we thought might go along with "Dow Farm," since there were stocks there. We weren't certain about the "Boone" part of the riddle, but we thought that Boone County, Nebraska might be too obvious. My husband did suggest that Boone might be in reference to Daniel Boone, a frontiersman, and therefore, Curtis (which is in Frontier County, Nebraska), might fit the riddle in that way, as well. We searched a long time, but we came up emptyhanded. It was chilly and extremely windy, so we decided to drive around the town a bit to look for alternate places to search. We ended up stopping to search at the high school football field, which also had many cement corners and was also located next to some cattle stocks. After not finding anything there, we grabbed some snacks, let the kids run around at the park for a while, and then took off for Beaver City. Beaver City was a little over an hour southeast of Curtis, and once we arrived there, it had gotten dark. Still, my husband and I took turns looking around the town's park with a flashlight and, after that, the fairgrounds, which had many cement corners and stocks. We also looked at a historical marker that was in the area. Then, we headed home, and decided we'd hunt again on Sunday, if the next riddle gave us any leads.

At noon on Sunday, we received the riddle, and we knew that we were on the right track by thinking about Baby Ruth candy bars. However, we mistakenly understood the second line of the new riddle to mean that we should drop the word "Baby" and focus only on "Ruth."

quick internet search told us that the name Ruth means "friend," and we knew there was a town Nebraska named Friend. So, on Sunday afternoon, we traveled around an hour and a half east hunt in Friend. We did think that "old sharpie" might be referencing a marker of some sort, so aybe a historical marker or a town sign or something. We searched around any likely spots in iend, but we didn't find anything. So, our kids played at the town park, and we headed back to earney.

nce the next day was Monday, my husband was going to be at work and my older two children school when the next riddle was released. We agreed that I'd go hunting with our youngest ild if Monday's riddle gave us any new leads. On Sunday night, I kept researching, and I became etty convinced that it had to be in Friend after all, or maybe in Albion, NE, a town in which we ad not searched, but which matched up with the riddles pretty well, I thought (stocks, baseball, oone County). On Monday morning, I drove east to Grand Island, NE so that I would have a head art to either Friend or Albion when the next riddle was released. I was parked in a gas station arking lot when we got the next riddle.

vasn't immediately sure what this meant, but I quickly decided it didn't help my Friend or Albion eas. My husband and I had been texting a little, and he suggested that "Tickertown" might mean ockville, NE or Stockham, NE. We also briefly considered Valentine, NE, which is known as ebraska's Heart City, since "ticker" might have been referencing "heart." With no clear answer, I eaded back west to Kearney, got our daughter some lunch, and kept thinking and texting with y husband. I texted that I was thinking about the Stockville historical marker, which is located on ie highway between Curtis and Stockville (and which we had driven right by on Saturday!). The hrase "I drove almost to Tickertown" made me think of the location of the marker on the ghway. My husband looked up the marker on Google Earth and could see that it was located ear some trees off the highway, and he texted me and said he thought it was a perfect match. I aded up quickly and left, and our daughter napped while I drove. Once I went through Stockville eading west, I knew the marker would soon be coming into sight. I was so relieved when I saw iat no other cars were parked there. I pulled over and looked around the corners of the cement ase of the marker until I saw a spot that looked promising. I used a stick to brush away the sandy oil, and I soon saw the top of the fake rock, and I knew I had found it! I got it out of the soil, and : that moment, a truck pulled up. I thought it was probably someone stopping to see if I was aving car trouble, but it was another hunter! He was extremely kind and gracious and ongratulated me on finding it. After he drove away, I got my daughter out of the van to let her ind" the treasure, too, and to take some photos. I then texted and called my husband to share ie good news!

verall, this was such a fun experience for us as a family. We had a great time travelling around ie state, researching and thinking and, of course, finding the gold ticket. We plan to use the prize ioney toward a future trip to Disney World, and we're looking forward to hunting for the candy ictory prize next year.

Nebraska
Memories

Nevada

Winner: Jamie Heintz

Green Belt Park Western Pacific - Elko, NV

Nov 28, 2020 at 12:00 pm - Nov 30, 2020 at 1:58 pm

Riddle:
ring ring ring got a call from Clearwater I took
a car broke down so we read the book
I'm ok and THE fire is out
like the lights? They are flashing about

Clue 1:
Oh Dear don't have an emergency
X marks the spot in this treasure urgency
100 years ago stripes were in
Green ones though would make you win

After waking up extremely early, our family (Ryan Heintz, Jamie Heintz, Mckenzie Heintz (age 11) and Madeline Heintz (age 7)) left our home in Northern California Saturday morning to arrive in Reno before the Nevada clue was released. We spent Saturday searching around the Reno/Sparks area and thought that the ring ring ring in the clue meant three springs. Late Saturday afternoon we thought for sure we had solved the riddle and it was a historical marker in Alamo about the Pahranagat Valley. The historical marker stated that three springs met Crystal Springs (Clearwater), Hinko (OK) and Ash (fire is out). The question mark in the clue led us to believe it was a historical marker. It is also near Area 51 and fit the lights flashing about.

Being convinced we had the right answer, after a couple hours of sleep, we left Reno at 12:30 a.m. and drove over 7 hours to Alamo. Part of our drive included a stretch on Highway 50 known as "The Loneliest Highway in America." Unfortunately, we were incorrect and headed towards Las Vegas. My husband started researching towns as we drove and once he pulled up an article about Elko and the Centennial Tower, he saw that it was "Chilton" Centennial Tower and he instantly knew we were right because of Chilton auto manuals. It also stated it was in Greenbelt Express Park, that the engineer was "Mark" Chilton and that the tower has marquee lights. Everything clicked perfectly. So, we once again started to race to our answer and crossed our fingers it wasn't found before we arrived. We were back on the loneliest highway for the second time that day. It was a long and anxious over six-hour drive to Elko.

We arrived at the Chilton Centennial Tower at 10:00 p.m. and it was 18 degrees. We started searching the tower itself, then the park and finally the train. After about fifteen minutes, I found the gold ticket in the train's undercarriage on a little ledge by ducking underneath part of the train and using a flashlight. We were so excited! On Sunday we had driven for over 20 hours criss crossing across the state from Reno, Alamo, Las Vegas, Indian Springs and finally Elko.

We found out that many teams had been there searching for hours before our arrival. So, we were extremely excited and grateful to have been the ones who found the gold ticket after a long but fulfilling adventure full of family fun. Our whole family had an amazing time and we are so thankful for the opportunity.

Nevada
Memories

NEW HAMPSHIRE

Winner: Nick Ryder

The Grand Trunk - Gorham, NH

Nov 7, 2020 at 10:00 am - Nov 10, 2020 at 1:31 pm

Riddle:
Charlie gave me 3 quarters
David gave me 3 silver dimes
Penny could care less about the money
She just wanted to go for a ride

Clue 1:
Casey wears numbers you'll see when there
I'm on display for all to stare
Reading my riddle could give you my city
Treasure hunting is fun and enjoy this ditty

Clue 2:
The Grand old man's in town with silver hair
Loved to wheel his wife around in a chair
They could see themselves in the fork and spoon
Check out the ledge under the edge at noon

Clue 3:
I FALL from above and love little towns
My grandpa Randy left me 2 SILVER pounds
Look under the ledge near the wheel
A rock held me down, so no one will STEEL

I first heard of The Candyman's national treasure hunt while gathering news stories for my podcast. David had been featured on several sites because of the attention-grabbing headline "Candymaker to Give Away a Factory!" Once I read the news on the show, I found David and Stephanie to be engaging and it was fun to follow their adventures through their Youtube channel. A friend and podcast listener, Tom, convinced me to enter us in the hunt for New Hampshire.

About 15 minutes before the riddle was set to release, I reminded Tom we were doing it. He'd forgotten the date! I formed a group online chat with him, my partner Sophie, and two other hunters, James and Andrew. At 10am I shared the riddle with my team, and chased a few early leads without success. The weather was perfect in New Hampshire this weekend and while the riddles were stumping us, I considered this adventure a good excuse for one or two days of some sightseeing and general driving. I was okay that I was not going to solve it.

Not for Tom though. He did not give up after ten hours on Saturday, when it was still not found. His hunger for Gold became insatiable. The hunt consumed him. He researched another eleven hours on Sunday, chasing lead after lead about famous skiers, baseball players, and King Odysseus. No longer did Tom's job, pets, or family matter. There was only the Gold Ticket.

Twelve hours on Monday.

Tuesday morning, he awakens the group chat: "Oh my gosh I think I found it! Going now!" A two and a half hour cross-state dash commenced toward the Gorham Historical Society and the Grand Trunk Railway, not stopping for even a bathroom. Tom arrived mere minutes before other teams and a frantic search for the Candyman's Ticket was underway. Not finding anything visible outside the train, Tom dove to the gravel, crawling between the tracks under locomotive 7531.

Searching every corner along the way, and finally spotted the smallest of rocks out of place: tucked out of sight above the wheel of the train car. Passed within feet by possibly hundreds of other searchers. He grabbed at the stone, and with it, the Gold Ticket pulled from its hiding spot, finally securing his victory, and ending one of the longest searches of them all.

NEW JERSEY

Winner: Kimberly & Hope Foley

Andover Borough Park - Andover, NJ

Oct 29, 2020 at 2:00 pm - Oct 29, 2020 at 4:14 pm

Riddle:
3 ducks were calm And 3 birds were cute
near this big rock is where you'll find the loot
Don't forget to take a fork to help cover up the school
Children will be screaming, happy time is absolutely
cool

Once upon a time..
A New Jersey family of 8 had a chance to figure out a riddle, perhaps a rhyme!
Although they are usually running late...
On October 27th they were right on time!

Who was on the hunt you ask?
5 Tie Dye Superheroes who were ready for the task!
River, Ryder & little brother Rain...
Sawyer and his big brother Shane!
We can't forget 2 Mom's who are sisters,
 Along with one mighty clever Mister!
Oh and one furry friend,
who was with them TIL the end!

Cars were packed...
Kids were snacked ...
Nothing could keep them off their track!

The riddle was out, ready to unlock!
3 ducks, 3 birds, a rock?
What could this all be?
What could this all mean?
The outcome is surely to be seen!

Their ideas were here, there & everywhere,
But nothing seemed to fit...
That's until the clever Mister thinks he has a hit!

Could one small word take them on their way?
Could one small word, make for a better day?

A n d?!? A n d?!!
Maybe it's a town that starts with A n d?
Let's see, let's see!
Andover they shout!!
Let's go!! Let's go!!
They've got this riddle figured out!

So off they flew!
Like true Super Heroes should do!
The entire ride there,
They googled, they giggled
They most certainly wiggled!

Are we there yet, the boys yell?
They were so ready for a tale to tell!

We're here! We're here!
So with their hearts full of glee!
And THE rock within their site!
They started to dig with all of their might!

Could it be? Could it be?
Is that GOLD they see?!?

Did this family of 8,
Actually claim their state!?!

Did they find the Gold Ticket...
Before anyone else could pick it?
Indeed they did!!!
Beneath the rock, the shiny Gold Ticket hid!

They screamed with pure joy...
For this prize was far better than any toy!

This was the best day ever they shouted!!
How could they even have doubted...
That with a wee bit of luck...
And a wee bit of smarts...
That this rainy day would live on forever in their hearts!

With many thanks to Stephanie & David...
these memories will never be faded!

Yours truly & truly yours!
The Tie Dye Super Heroes!

New Jersey Memories

The Gold Ticket!

NEW MEXICO

Winner: Kristine Goddard

Journey's End Sculptures - Santa Fe, NM

Dec 12, 2020 at 10:00 am - Dec 14, 2020 at 3:07 pm

Riddle:
My watch told me to get my filling
A week is what I needed now so I was really thrilling
Ray was the one who showed me, the lead one he did love
Look under a little uppity spot, and 4" with a shove....L(sorry, it didn't rhyme so well, but we're at the finishing line)

Clue 1:
There are 4 stages of riddle solving
Some folks thinking is evolving
Some want a riddle rider
My favorite is to be the canon hider

Clue 2:
Nick is coming over, make sure your shirts are pressed nice
I don't want you to stop believing that many paid a heavy price
All who said the ground might be frozen, remember treasure hunters must thrive
Dig 4" under the the correct one, and you'll walk away with five
Nota-e photo of tha ectuel locetion would giva too much ewey. Just esk Ray.

Our journey to The Golden Ticket as told by Kristine aka twin B:

It all began when I saw a Facebook post talking about a treasure hunt and candy factory. I was immediately intrigued, and I told my twin sister Grace and our Dad about it that day. I purchased a ticket for my state on September 9th• I was so excited, little did I know we would be the last state to go. Waiting about killed me! I could not wait, so I bought a ticket for another state. My husband and kids drove with me to Colorado. We had hopes high and great. We drove six hours the wrong way, until the candy man acknowledged our mistake. We saw hot springs and mountains and a lake, so all was not lost in our little escapade.

Day one:

The day finally come, and I was up early. I drove over to my sister's house with my two girls Audrey (age 7) and Katie (age 8). The mini van was gassed up and filled with treasure hunting essentials such as snacks, shovel, videos to entertain the kids on the drive. The riddle was released, and within five minutes I had figured out the town!! ! Or so I thought. I thought the first line in the riddle was about the "filling"= dentist and second line, "a week is what I needed"= days off ... vacation ... holiday ... Dentist and Holiday .. .hmmm. My twin said , "watch=clock=doc" ... Ericka 'Doc Holliday'. So off we went to Las Vegas New Mexico, a town where Doc Holliday once owned a saloon. The rest of the riddle did not make since, but we had 3 and ½ hours to figure it out. One glitch in the plan, no internet signal for almost the entire drive ... agh.

Three hours into the drive, my kids wanted no part in looking for a golden ticket and driving all day again. The constant whining, "are we there yet", "how much longer" prompted me to call my parents who live near Santa Rosa to meet us on the cutoff and have some quality grandparent time with the grandkids.

On the way to Las Vegas, after dropping off the non- enthusiastic hunters, my sister Grace decided to drive and within 10 minutes of driving she got pulled over for speeding. She conveniently forgot her purse \\ driver licenses ... This reminded me of a time when we both first got our license. I was such a careful driver and Grace not so much. She had and still has a bit of a led foot. She got so many tickets her first year driving, one more and she would have lost her license. So what do you think my sister did? Stop driving like a maniac? No she took my license and starting putting tickets on it! So here we are almost 30 years later, and she used my license again. Haha!

We arrived at high noon in Las Vegas armed with a metal detector, shovel, and cute outfits, we awaited a shot out with other treasure hunters. To our surprise no other hunters were there. We searched for hours and found nothing. Grace looked at me, and said "I hope it wasn't in Pie town".

On a whim, we decided to bead towards Raton because it is the last town on the boarder of Colorado and we thought maybe the part in the riddle "finish line" met state line. We searched Raton and found nothing. Defeated, we beaded back toward Las Vegas, but on the way back, we saw a sign for Cimarron. We could not decide if we should go there and so we missed the turn off. As we were researching Cimarron a town named Rayado was near it, and then the part of the riddle talking about Ray made us think maybe it was this town! Only one problem we would have to turn around because we missed the turn off, or did we??? My good old trusty Google map said there was a back road to Rayado and so we took it. The road started at mile marker one, a good sign right? An even better sign was that the pavement stopped and it became a dirt road. My sister who has a much better since of direction then I, said "we should turn around" ... This reminds me of another time when I was driving us back home from Alaska to New Mexico, and I got us lost in bush country far far into the mountains of Alaska. I had apparently missed our tum and drove on a snowmobile path through a river and strait to a loge that no ever drives

into; They only fly into it! I'll never forget that lady's face when I pulled up in my little Yugo car. So naturally this dirt road to Rayado did not scare me, I bad driven worse ... But as we started up a step cliff, I did began to wonder if my sister was right? Hmmm... no where to turn around now. Up we went. On the positive side the view was beautiful and when we got to the top there were herds of Pronghorn antelope! Time to turn around, and back down we went to the highway again. We decided to back track and take the correct turn off. By the time we arrived to Rayado it was almost dark and the museum was closed. Wild turkeys were in the trees ready to roost and I also was getting very tired at this point. Off we went to pick up my kids and head home. By the time day one was done, and I got home it was 1 am the only thing waiting up for our return was our two kittens. We hoped day two's clue would reveal the riddles secrets.

Day 2:

I barely slept, because I keep thinking about the riddle all night. My kids and husband were fast asleep. I woke my husband up and said, "I'm off to my sister's", "have fun watching the kids". He wished me luck and I wished him luck.

Next days clue came out and as we looked at my sister and I said out loud, "four stages" "stage coach!!!" . This new clue sent us into a new direction! My Dad who was on our team and whom had not contributed much in the way of research, was very helpful on the second day. We all started looking at the history of the. stage coach, Santa Fe trail, and then I thought four stages maybe the fourth stage coach stop? But I was still stuck on my Doc Holliday thought process, Las Vegas was one of the stops but not the last stop. Time to rethink, my Dad thought it might be in Raton, but my sister and I had already been there so we did not want to drive up there again. The part in the riddle that talked about "Show Me" reminded me of the slogan for Missouri "the show me state". The Santa Fe trail did have something to do with Missouri and all. So off we went to the trails end, Santa Fe New Mexico. The first part of the riddle we thought now met, "filling =gold filling, and watch was clock". There is a large golden clock in Santa Fe. The next line "seven days" was solved by our Dad who said, "it took seven days for the stage coach to travel from Denver to Santa Fe". We figured it was in Santa Fe, and as we researched more, my sister came across "Journeys End" a statue by Reynaldo Rivera. All the pieces were coming together. We went to the Museum hill in Santa Fe. We thought the statue was located by the cafe on museum hill but it wasn't. We finally found the location of the statue. We got out with our large shovel and metal detector in hand and headed to the lead horse. We figured it has to be the lead horse, because of the part in the riddle that slated, "the lead one he did love". The ground was so hard, we tried our hardest to dig, but the dirt barely moved. It was like concrete. We then thought lets put water on the dirt to see if that would warm it up. Off to the nearest gas station we went, and we returned with five gallons of water. We poured water on the spot, we tried and tried. Nothing worked the ground was frozen solid. We decided to take a video to show how frozen the ground was. We sent our email and video to the tricky treasure people. There was nothing else we could do. Home we went.

Day 3:

We knew we had to try to go back and dig at Journeys End as soon as the sun had warmed up the place. We left latter in the day and headed towards Santa Fe. About an hour from Santa Fe we got a call from the Candy Man telling us that the police had been called and now the site was considered inaccessible. Since we were the first to claim the correct location with video proof that we could not retrieve it, we were awarded the prize. Our journey for this hunt has come to an end, but with every ending come a new beginning! Happy Hunting tootsie twins!

New Mexico Memories

NEW YORK

Winner: Devon Meenagh

Welcome New Windsor Est.1763 - New Windsor, NY

Nov 7, 2020 at 2:00 pm - Nov 9, 2020 at 5:16 pm

Riddle:
To visit you must leave Little Arch yes in deed
Look up nearby and give it a read
Don't take too much time or change things so drastic
It's below the right post, you'll think it's fantastic

Clue 1:
Little Arch is really a cute guy
Come to this place and wave hello and hi
The side you will stop, when you are leaving
It's by a post not a tree and the doc's work can be
deceiving

Clue 2:
HW+MW=AW
Don't drive through the red light, I care
The post is square and you're pulled off here
It's not in NYC or Long Island, so don't go there

I found out about the hunt on Twitter. I don't have a car, I'm bad with directions, and thanks to the Pandemic I barely had $50, so I did what any struggling millennial adult would do: called my dad. After a bit of convincing, throwing out words like "adventure", "memories", and "five thousand dollars", he agreed to go half-in on a ticket with me. I've lived in New York City for the past 10 years, formerly from Duchess County where my family still lives. We've always loved brain teasers, puzzles, mysteries, and I've personally conquered half the escape rooms in NY. It seemed like a perfect fit for us, and in an already absurd year, why not throw in a fantastical treasure hunt run by a cheerful Candyman?

When the clue dropped at 2pm on Saturday, we were sitting at the kitchen table with every WiFi-enabled device we owned out and ready to research. Our shoes were on, the car was over-packed, and my mom and brother had been recruited to help. In under an hour, my dad and I were at a cemetery in Hyde Park. We had zeroed in on "Little Arch" and this cemetery was the burial place for a man named Archibald Rogers' son, Archie Jr. who had died young (don't take too much time). After that we headed to the actual Rogers' estate, (in deed could refer to land) but it was now private property. We went to the library and the historical society (look up nearby and give it a read) still chasing down Archibald Rogers' family, and took a stroll through FDR's estate down the road (there was an Archibald Roosevelt in the family) before realizing we were already out of ideas. When we got home we wrote out the riddle on a giant white board and sat it in the middle of the kitchen where we could stare at it. We researched every famous Archie/Archibald we could find, including Archie Comics, which could get you to Riverdale OR to Mamaroneck where Archie comics is headquartered. We even did research on Prince Archie, and found a town named Little Britain, as well as roads with names like "Prince St", but nothing we were finding felt solid enough to physically chase down.

Around midnight, on a map of NY we found a tiny town called Archville - to visit you must leave Little Arch, if you leave Archville you end up in the town of Sleepy Hollow. Given the infamous Legend of Sleep Hollow (give it a read) we started thinking about Washington Irving, who also wrote Rip Van Winkle (don't take too much time or change things so drastic- look up the story). I pulled an all-nighter researching the famous landmarks of Sleepy Hollow and by noon on Sunday, we had already visited the Headless Horseman Bridge, Washington Irving's Monument, his grave site, the Headless Horseman Statue, Washington Irving's Estate, and the "Welcome to Sleepy Hollow" sign. When the hint was released at 2pm, we were sitting in the Sleepy Hollow cemetery eating sandwiches and we weren't ready to give up on Sleepy Hollow yet.

We made connections in the new hint to the lighthouse, the boat club, the hospital, and a few other spots. We even made our way back to the "Welcome to Sleepy Hollow" sign (wave hello or hi) which still didn't match the post pictured no matter how long we stared at it. Again, we went home empty-handed, and again, I pulled an all-nighter. On Monday, my dad had to go back to work, so my mom joined me, and we were back in Sleepy Hollow by 9am that morning. We decided to go back because Sleepy Hollow used to be called "North Tarrytown" but they changed the name in the 90s: "don't take too much time (don't TARRY)". This time we really focused on the new hint, especially "the doc's work can be deceiving". We had correctly guessed that this could refer to a plastic surgeon at this point, but we couldn't connect it to Sleepy Hollow. We went to the visitor's center at the park, the Tarrytown historical society (in deed - they keep historical documents there), the library (give it a read) and a few other landmarks and parks for good measure. When we left Sleepy Hollow, we were confident that it wasn't there.

When the second hint was released, we immediately made the connection to Prince Archie again, and the "Ws" in the equation helped it to finally click: Archie Windsor, the NEW Windsor. With the new details, we were positive that it would be somewhere near the edge of the town right off the road where you would leave (to visit you must leave), so we started driving around that edge. We had tried googling "New Windsor Welcome sign" (wave hello or hi) but didn't find anything. We pulled over at least 40 times so I could jump out and check random sign posts, flag poles, and fence posts. The phrase "I care" got us back onto doctors and plastic surgeons, so we stopped at a center for cosmetic surgery and a dentist, as well as a few optometrists (I care, eyecare), all near red lights like the hint mentioned. We knew what we were looking for, we just didn't know where it was. As we made our way around the outside of town, we left no stone unturned, stopping at Storm King Sculpture Garden, the Temple Hill monument, and Knox Headquarters, and every interesting post by the road in between. We had just left Knox headquarters and were headed to another landmark on the North edge of the town when we stopped at a red light. That's when we spotted it: the elusive Welcome to New Windsor sign, and right next to it, a giant billboard for Dr. Fugo, cosmetic surgeon. A ton of cars were passing by for rush hour and we didn't want to draw too much attention, so my mom waited in the car while I took my garden shovel and dug and found...nothing. Thankfully, I had the good sense to then try digging on the OTHER side of the post. After 3 days of no sleep, very few food breaks, driving around for hours, and at least a hundred wrong locations, I saw a glint of gold 5 inches down, exactly like they said. In that moment, kneeling on the side of the road in the dirt, in the dark, I felt like Arthur pulling the sword out of the stone — except he probably didn't cry as much.

New York Memories

NORTH CAROLINA

Winner: Peter Raines

Lions Park - Cary, NC

Oct 14, 2020 at 11:00 am - Oct 15, 2020 at 12:06 pm

Riddle:
The crook in the tree carried the creatures all in black
I couldn't catch a break, nor could I slack.
If the coward bit me while I seek
I'd pee my pants before I shriek.

Clue 1:
It was 8:15 am when Carrie woke up and stretched as
high as possible into the air
Her hair was all tangled and she used the wooden
hair brush that hardly did a thing.
It was time for her little brother's game and she didn't
really want to go.
So instead...she packed up the car, jumped in and
went to find treasure!

This is the story of how my best friend and I found the golden necklace in North Carolina. I first learned about the Gold Ticket through my mom, who sent me a news article about it in September. I like supporting cool ideas, so I bought a ticket, even knowing that I was unlikely to find it, considering that 1,000 people in each state had a shot. I live in central NC, so if it were at the beach, or in the mountains, it would be an even longer shot because of the distance to get to it from here.

So time went by and the day of the riddle for NC came up. I stopped everything that I was doing at 11:00 am when it was released. And then... I had no idea what to do with it. It was confusing, and it led to so many places, from nearby parks all the way out to the Wizard of Oz park in western NC. It felt like I could make everything fit the riddle. I went to a local park that could kind of sort of be made to fit the riddle, and got a nice 2 mile hike in. But no necklace was there.

My teammate, Gary, was equally confused after reading the riddle later in the day when he was done with work. So we waited, knowing that someone else would figure it out first.

And then, at 11 am the next day, the clue was released. And that made all the difference - both the riddle and the clue referenced versions of Cary (misspelled as Carrie), which is a town about 15 minutes away from me (and an hour away from my teammate). I did my Google sleuthing and zoomed in on Cary, and saw several spots that jumped out - nothing more than words in the riddle and clue that lined up with roads and parks in the city. And then it hit both of us at the same time - we were looking right at it. Or at least where it was generally hidden - Lions Park in Cary, NC.

I told Gary that I was heading out to see if it was there. He suggested grabbing lunch first and searching after, but I knew it would be gone if we waited, so I jumped in my car and told him I would meet him for lunch after I took a quick look there. I was there at the park by 11:22 am. And... no one was there. Not a soul other than myself and a few groundskeepers.

I was on the phone with a client as I pulled into the parking lot, and so I had to tell them that something came up and I would have to call them back. Ah... not my proudest moment there, but I had to get out of the car and search before anyone else showed up.

The riddle mentioned a tree, so I thought it would be high up in a tree somewhere, and started looking around, wondering if I should have brought a ladder. I started walking through the park , stopping at all of the trees along the way, with very little else to go on.

As luck would have it, a municipal truck was parked in front of a small building, and it drove away after a few minutes, showing that the building was a public restroom - and the riddle mentioned peeing, so I walked over to the building. I saw a small tree next to the restrooms, in a landscaped area along a sidewalk, and I walked up to it, feeling more excited with every step.

I walked up to the tree, and stood against it, on my tip toes. I could see, sitting in the tree, just above my eye level, in the crook between branches, a very clean rock, the size of a child's hand. It was a rock sitting in a tree, which was very much out of place. I started to feel a bit lightheaded as I reached in and lifted up the rock to find the necklace sitting underneath it.

I picked it up and looked at it. I felt like I was standing outside my body while I stared at the necklace. I knew that I had to leave, but didn't want to drive. I took a quick photo of the necklace and sent it to Gary, and then looked around.

Two cars were pulling into the gravel parking lot and driving by me. A group of people were walking up the sidewalk with phones out, very deliberately looking in the grass, like an Easter egg hunt. Someone was in the park across the street, walking through a baseball field.

I had an iron grip on the necklace and refused to even put it in my pocket as I walked past the people getting out of their cars, and got into mine.

I felt ecstatic, and I felt bad. I didn't want them to search in vain, but I also didn't want to yell out that I had it. So I waited until I could drive and left the park, now full of people, and drove a block over to pull over in the parking lot of a small shop.

That's when I emailed in the code and got a nearly immediate response, asking if I would be ok getting interviewed on YouTube live. I had run out of my house without even showering or getting properly dressed! But I said okay and, thankfully, it was a phone call and not a video interview.

Since I didn't take pictures or videos as I was searching (I snapped a few of some of the trees when I first got out of the car, but forgot about it once I saw the tree that I thought it was in. lol), they asked me to go back and take a few. So of course I did.

And so I drove through the parking lot that was now full of people and cars, and parked, and got out, and walked towards the spot where I found it, still gripping it in my hand. And I saw that the interview was being watched by almost everyone in the park, which felt bad, because so many families and kids were out searching for the necklace.

By the time I got to the tree, most of the people were in the process of leaving. And I took a few candid photos of the tree and the spot, and reset the necklace to take photos of it in the tree, without making a scene of it.

And that's when someone yelled out to me from across the street that the necklace had been found, and I paused and then replied that I knew that it had. And they said "hey, are you the guy who found it!?" and I said "um... Yes..." and then they came up and chatted with me and we took photos together and we all talked for a while about the contest and where we looked and life and everything. And a few more people showed up and joined the crowd, which was lovely. I have many new Facebook friends and I am thankful for those connections!

In the end, I was there for quite some time, and my friend and teammate, Gary, was ever so patiently waiting to eat lunch with me and share the excitement. So off I went, to celebrate a wonderful adventure with new and old friends alike.

NORTH DAKOTA

Winner: Stephanie Arbach

Steamboat Park - Bismarck, ND

Oct 24, 2020 at 2:00 pm - Oct 24, 2020 at 2:57 pm

Riddle:
Samuel and or Mark knew where to go
and Steve sang he did too.
They both would be very gentle
when they looked inside the flue

My name is Stephanie Arbach and I'm from Bismarck, North Dakota. I found out about The Gold Ticket treasure hunt on my Facebook newsfeed. After I did some initial researching, I got really excited as I love riddles and thought it sounded like a great way to have an adventure. Since I work full-time and have 4 children, I decided to ask my 18-year old stepdaughter, Kassidy, and my best friend, Allyson, if they wanted to do the hunt with me and we could have a girls weekend. They loved the idea so we marked it on our calendar. I even made us matching shirts for the big day. A week before our scheduled riddle release date, Allyson ended up in isolation due to COVID. Kassidy and I decided to still do the hunt and Allyson would help us virtually.

An hour before the riddle release, Kassidy and I filled up the vehicle and loaded up with snacks from the gas station. Before the riddle was released, I had thought it would be in a smaller city based on previous states. Once the riddle released, I was completely stumped. We decided to just stay at home and do some research. Based on the image, my husband wondered if it wasn't possibly down on River Road as there are lots of various statues. At this point, we had no other leads so we decided to go check it out. As I was pulling out of my driveway, Allyson texted and said the first line was definitely in reference to Mark Twain.

I texted my husband about Mark Twain and he immediately said, "steamboat" and proceeded to tell me he was grabbing the 3 kids and was going to come. On River Road, there is a Steamboat Park. At this point, I was becoming excited so we took off on the 10 minute drive from my house to Steamboat Park. On the drive there, Kassidy was researching Steamboat Park and showed me an image of an eagle statue and said she thought it could be in the wing. After reviewing the image, I started to get really excited that we had it. When we arrived, there was no one else there so we quickly got out and went to the statue. After looking up in one of the wings, I saw some small gold beads. I could not believe it and told Kassidy, "Oh my gosh! We found it!". However, due to the cold weather, it was frozen so we had to go to the vehicle and get a pen to wiggle it loose so we could get it out.

Just as we retrieved it, my husband pulled in with the 3 small kids. He was in total shock that we found it. My 7- year old was over the moon excited for the necklace and asked if she could keep it. Even though we found it quick – around 25 minutes after the riddle release – it was definitely a quick adventure and I was glad my children got to be apart of it. A lady arrived 5 minutes after my husband and asked if she could take our picture. Her pure excitement for us made me even more excited for the win. My favorite part of the whole thing was when I was being interviewed live on YouTube and David asked me what I was going to do with the $5,000, Kassidy's eyes got big. When I got off the interview, she proceeded to ask how much I won. Apparently, I never told her what the value of the necklace was and she was just excited for the girls weekend. The next day, we headed over to Allyson's house to get a picture with her, socially distanced, of course!

North Dakota Memories

OKLAHOMA

Winner: Johnny Sandmann

Vendome Well - Sulpher, OK

Dec 12, 2020 at 11:00 am - Dec 12, 2020 at 12:34 pm

Riddle:
I drove 233 miles to have good luck
I prefer a little fowl over a duck
Look for the lone boulder and look below
Find a gold ticket near your toe

Johnny Sandmann purchased his entry into the Oklahoma hunt as a gift for his wife, Tara, who has always had a fascination with treasurer hunts. When they embarked on the hunt, they initially thought the clue might be pointing to a casino near a mile marker 233 but thought that would be too obvious and take them too long to arrive. The girls were already anxious from driving and wanted to get out and look so they decided to go to the park in Sulphur and let them run around looking under rocks. Tara initially thought the word fowl could be an anagram for foul smell and the Sulphur water at the park has an obnoxious odor. About half-way there the clue began to make more sense. A small fowl could mean "Chick" and the park is called the Chickasaw National Recreation Area. Additionally it is across from the Artesian Casino which would point to the "good luck" part of the clue. Finally, Tara searched the internet for Sulphur and 233 and learned that Highway 177 running through Sulphur is exactly 233 miles long and ends just south of there in Madill, Oklahoma. Once arriving at the park, they found a single rock near the fountain. Unfortunately they did not think to bring a digging tool. Armed with some sticks and a plastic paintbrush they found in the car, they were able to unearth the necklace at 11 :21 a.m.

Johnny Sandmann is an Attorney, practicing real estate law in Coalgate and Atoka Oklahoma. He and his brother own Sonny's Grocer/ and Market in Coalgate and Wewoka. Tara works part-time at the law office and helps care for the young family.

OREGON

Winner: Josh Crawford

Grave Creek Covered Bridge - Wolf Creek, OR

Oct 29, 2020 at 4:00 pm - Oct 29, 2020 at 5:00 pm

Riddle:
Josie came upon this place, she's small and very cute
When she died she took pictures, and loved to honk and hoot
Go down by the post and move the gravel lightly
You will soon find me, I'm rather gold and brightly

We had heard about the hunt just a few days after it had hit the news. We live in Redding, CA. I'm a volunteer firefighter and a stay at home dad. We had gotten to work on the riddle and figured out what county it was in. We also figured out grave creek using the riddle and everything else just fell into place. We had been to the bridge before, so I was able to visualize the bridge. While we were there we did see fellow searchers and were congratulated. Others had missed the find by minutes from what we had seen. Our team consisted of my wife, daughter, my mother and sister. This was truly a one of a kind experience and has brought joy to 2020 in the most special way possible.

Oregon
Memories

OHIO

Winner: Mark Raab

Wordens Ledges - Hinckley, OH

Oct 29, 2020 at 12:00 pm - Oct 29, 2020 at 1:24 pm

Riddle:
Correct me if I'm wrong and give me an a instead of o.
I can't stop drinking in this place you maybe know
I face this special place, but there's no need to hike me
Find the pine tree near the car and 2" down you'll see

CANDYMAN'S TREASURE HUNT

Hi, my name is Mark Raab, and I am the winner of Ohio's Golden Ticket! I live on the east side of Cleveland with my partner Stan and our 11-year-old daughter Lilly. I have always enjoyed solving problems and riddles, both in my personal and professional life. For most of my career, I've worked in quality assurance for different medical device companies, where I have specialized in investigations and problem solving. Luckily, this means my coworkers have similar passions, which is how I met Tony Certo. Tony has worked with me for over 3 years, and even though we work for a New Jersey based company, he is also a local Ohioan. Tony lives on the west side of Cleveland with his wife, Jessica, and 1-year old son Joseph. When traveling for work, our team always looks for trivia nights or escape rooms as team building exercises. So when I first learned about The Gold Ticket treasure hunt, I knew we had to be a part of it.

In preparation for the hunt, I blocked off my afternoon work calendar, not knowing how long it would take us. When I read the words "face" and "hike" in the third line, I immediately remembered hiking a long time ago at a trail in Hinkley known for having faces carved into the sandstone. A quick search brought up Worden's Ledges. Tony and I discussed whether the location fit the rest of the riddle, and we decided to match at least one other part of the clue before making the drive.

Tony had not heard of Worden's Ledge before, and fortunately, upon searching for it using online maps, misspelled it "Warden". This brought up police and sheriff location results which helped us link the location to the first line of the clue – Warden, with an "a" instead of an "o" as a "correctional" officer. With two lines of the clue matching, we raced to the location.

In addition to the riddle, the clue also included a picture of a tree, and we studied the look of the white bark and many low, horizontal branches. When we arrived, we saw a lone tree with white bark and low, horizontal branches in the middle the small L shaped parking lot. Not having a shovel, Tony scraped at the ground using a snow brush from the trunk of his car, searching for golden ticket. I had to point out to him the tree picture also included a red circle on exactly where to dig, but because Tony is color-blind, he had missed it. Now on the right spot, two scoops of the ice scraper revealed the chain of the dog tag. We could not believe we had actually found the golden ticket! Sadly, walking back to the car another vehicle pulled in with someone who surely would have won if we were even a few minutes later. Within the hour, we were on the phone with The Candyman himself celebrating our victory and discussing Cleveland Indians baseball.

PENNSYLVANIA

Winner: Scott Reed

Friendship Tree Keystone Park - Bath, PA

Nov 7, 2020 at 3:00 pm - Nov 8, 2020 at 5:56 pm

Riddle:
Jolly went as fast as can be
Make some friends with some leaves you see
I'm directly behind this cold metal bench
Dig down 4" but don't make a trench

Clue 1:
The man at the corner likes what you've grown
He doesn't like water in his eyes or he'll moan
Do they make bombs here in this nice place?
If you know The Candyman, he'd make this his base

Our team consisted of myself, Scott Reed, my wife Crystal Reed, and my brother and his wife Matt and Laura Reed. We both live in Pennsylvania and pretty much have lived here our entire lives. We live about an hour apart from each other. I was the first to hear of the contest and I immediately called my brother and decided this was definitely something we wanted to do. We bought two tickets, one for Maryland(we live about 15 minutes from MD border) and one for Pennsylvania.

We had no success on the Maryland hunt, but the entire experience had us completely excited for the Pennsylvania hunt. When the clue first dropped we were completely puzzled. We really had no clue and had driven around to a few longshot ideas and none paid off so we decided we would regroup the next day and get started in the morning. The next day we searched to no avail all morning and anxiously awaited to see if there would be a new clue that and there was. My wife and I had a birthday party to go to that afternoon but I was on the phone with my brother the whole time talking and discussing ideas. His wife was the one that came up with Bath, Pa from the bomb clue. She grew up about 20 minutes from Bath and thought it might be a reference. Upon searching Bath in maps we discovered that there was a park in Bath on the corner of Green and Race streets (Both references in the clue from the previous day).

Once I Googled the park and found out that it was home to America's friendship tree(Another clue from the previous day)I told my brother "Start driving there right now". People at the party thought I was crazy because I began dancing around in the yard yelling "we know where it is!". I yanked my wife from the party and we jumped in our car to head there as well. My brother was about an hour away from the park in Bath and they arrived first and called me immediately when they found the gold ticket. I couldn't believe it. We raced to meet them and needless to say it was one of the best experiences we have ever had. It was great getting to spend time with family and take on a different kind of challenge. We're eternally grateful for the opportunity.

RHODE ISLAND

Winner: Seth Mandeville

Miller Waite Evans Memorial Park - North Providence, RI

Oct 17, 2020 at 3:00 pm - Oct 19, 2020 at 4:01 pm

Riddle:
4" below is a special tree north you know
We have a picture to show you so you don't go too low
Oxygen creates future protection of roots as did this man
Don't play around too long or we'll call you Tarzan

Clue 1:
I didn't dunk a donut in my beer
It's not in a cemetery so don't go there.
Do you go North or South, only you will know
I think you'll like why this tree did grow

Clue 2:
Dale couldn't hurry up because she had already been drinking
Her horse didn't understand what she was thinking
The kids loved to play so don't go where they can not
Mosey on over to just the right spot

The day the riddle came out, we had a couple of solid ideas that didn't pan out. When the hint came out we were even more lost, until I found what we thought was a big clue in downtown Providence. Trinity Brewhouse is directly across from the Dunkin Donuts center. Outside is a 95 North/South sign. So we figured it was north of Providence. When the second clue came out we googled "Dale and her horse" and Dale Evans and Buttermilk came up in our search. I searched for Evans Park. Evans Playground and a park in NORTH Providence came up. The park is 2 miles from my house. We lined up the picture with the tree and the flagpole and dug with our bare hands to find the Gold Ticket. We were over the moon. We said we were going to find it when we bought out ticket, and we did. What a fantastic weekend we had!!! We also tried for New Hampshire but we weren't as lucky, but had just as much fun. Thank you all so much for this amazing experience!!

SOUTH CAROLINA

Winner: Meghan Schindler

Tuskegee Airmen Memorial - Walterboro, SC

Oct 20, 2020 at 11:28 am - Oct 20, 2020 at 6:59 pm

Riddle:
Walter Anderson's arm was sure red
Becoming an adult he might dread
His small simple house you will know
Move Northwest and a way, aglow

I decided to buy a Golden Ticket after having hit all the Geo Caches in our town with the kids and missing the thrill of hearing all the stories from my sisters who went searching for the Fenn Treasure. I was beyond thrilled when I had seen the Facebook Ad with David's Face surrounded by Jelly Beans!

Our boots on the ground team was my daughter, Maisie (who I was so excited wasn't too cool for this), my son Bo, who looking back at our win, I'm so glad needed to get out of the car to burn some energy... He played a role in us getting to the Tuskagee Airmen Memorial before checking out another spot first! And my husband James who couldn't stop Cruising up and down ALT 17, Cottageville HWY. Special thanks to our lead detectives, they were a big help with even bigger imaginations!!

We are forever grateful for these special memories!!

The Yadlosky Family

Our entire family is basically over the top crazy when it comes to riddles, puzzles, games of any kind! When my daughter came home in September and had heard about the hunt from her school librarian, we signed up immediately!

We recruited my two sister's families--ironically, my Mother's daughters--for our team. We had my uncle and cousin on clue help as well.

Day 1: My family took off about 2 hours ahead of riddle release with a plan to drive toward my hometown of Miller which is fairly East central with routes to Spearfish, Lemmon, or Mobridge if needed. Youngest sister would be NE, Oldest sister would be SE. It took us about 45 minutes to crack Sisseton. Luckily, youngest sister actually lives right there!! We were between Nicollet Tower and the new roundabouts. They searched all over those 2 spots + every other crazy Sisseton stretch connection we could all come up with when those weren't panning out. My family arrived in Miller and we got to have lunch and visit with my Grandma. When a couple hours had passed and they hadn't found it we had to make a tough decision. Do we go NE and help them continue looking because we're 90% sure we've at least got Sisseton right, or do we go West following our next best lead of Belle Fourche? (Belle and "che" are both feminine, "Four" rounds, and four directions on the compass). We had confidence in my sister and went west. Night came and they had to give up.

Day 2: We knew immediately we had missed it yesterday in the search! Youngest sister got back there within 10 minutes, thinking they'd find it and still make church! Oldest sister hit the road to join them, thinking they'd arrive in a couple hours to celebrate together. Since we were already waaaay west, my family still went to check out the Geographical Center of the US - both the monument and the real one, because that was part of the adventure of this all too!! Saw a cool place we'd never been, and likely won't ever get back to. Uncle went to Faulkton right away this morning pre-clue release to cover that stretch idea.

Day 2 Afternoon: When all of yesterday's searchers had scoured and scoured and scoured again, oldest sister's family shows up with fresh eyes and motivation. Brother-in-law had actually scraped through the wheel dirt right away when they got there. After 2-3 hours of looking, bakery warm-up breaks, even walking as far as 3 blocks away to check the viewpoint from a flashing amber street light, they were about to go look across the street when one last pass through the tires and THERE IT WAS!

We all had so much fun working together on this. THANK YOU Dave and Stephanie for providing this opportunity. I said we wouldn't do any other states, but the riddle bug definitely has us, and I think we might convince my snowbird aunt and uncle to do AZ! We have been brainstorming the rest of the afternoon, and coming up with how we can continue to pay our good luck forward. Our dad would have LOVED doing this with us!

SOUTH DAKOTA

Winner: Sheila Brown

Veterans Memorial Tank - Sisseton, SD

Nov 14, 2020 at 11:00 am - Nov 15, 2020 at 2:36 pm

Riddle:
My mother's daughter was my best friend
She could lift an elephant till the very end
Round and round and round and round
No need to dig, as I'm not in the ground

Clue 1:
Time to make the donuts in a roundabout way
The horses love you and say neigh neigh
Watch for the star it's light and bold
Just like the ticket that's bright and gold

South Dakota
Memories

TENNESSEE

Winner: Tony Youngblood

Clear Fork River Gorge RR Crossing - Jellico, TN

Oct 8, 2020 at 11:00 am - Oct 10, 2020 at 2:34 pm

Riddle:
The first girl on the scene wouldn't cross, but heard
the screams of those we lost.
While eating gelatin and plastic ware and getting
drunk over there.
Look straight down below the light.
No shovel needed to know you're right.

Clue 1:
Dolly won't help you
Neither will the Titanic
It's not a crowded place
Look for a rock type case

Clue 2:
No Pigeon, no Nashville,
not a crowded place.
You might not ever heard of me,
is what maybe the case.

I first heard of the Gold Ticket through a treasure hunting Facebook group. After watching the Candyman documentary, I knew I had to try in our state of Tennessee. My team consisted of me, my wife Erica Ciccarone, and her work friend J.R. Lind, a 2-time champion on the TV show Jeopardy. When the riddle was released, it made me think of large scale tragedies, so I started looking up earthquakes, fires, and train wrecks. When I discovered the troop train derailment in Jellico, TN (Jellico = Jello = gelatin), I felt we were on the right track. Then I noticed the nearby Clear Fork River (plastic ware), and things were heating up. J.R. noticed a nearby railroad crossing and made the connection with the two parallel streets (Eve Ln = the first girl on the scene, Tipple Ln = to get drunk), and that cinched it. We figured it was under the railroad crossing light because the clue said to "look under the light." This all happened on day 1.

Now the only problem was getting there. We live in Nashville, and Jellico is 4 hours away. My boss surprised me with a "must do now task" for two days in a row. My wife and I decided that if it hadn't been found by the third day, a Saturday, we would get up early and drive to Jellico.

For the entire drive, I was biting my knuckles, worried that someone would beat us there. On the night before, someone had posted a picture of the Jellico troop train derailment site on the FB group, just a quarter mile from where we believe the necklace was hidden, and I was sure they'd find it before us. When we arrived in town, we went straight to the railroad crossing and started searching. After 45 seconds, my hand felt a rock that did not feel like stone. It felt like ... plastic! I yelled to my wife to come over and we flipped the rock over. Underneath was a door. We opened it and found the necklace!

It felt amazing, but I honestly was still so nervous that I didn't celebrate until we got a confirmation from David. Less than half an hour later, we were live chatting with David and Stephanie who confirmed we won!

We split the prize money three ways, after taxes, and now we have our sights set on the candy factory!

TEXAS

Winner: Kati Tucker

Old Sugarloaf Bridge - Gause, TX

Dec 5, 2020 at 11:00 am - Dec 8, 2020 at 7:37 am

Riddle:
Tom ate the big apple on his way
Walking over the small leak he goes today
Go two blocks and you will see
below some dirt is the key

Clue 1:
I'm not near El Paso or Amarillo now
I'm not very popular so don't say oh wow!
I'm near a crossing of water you see
Two Four Six really confuses me

Clue 2:
All good sons eat uno
School gave me a headache you know
Grab me a cookie on your way
You little hunter won't pay

The Texas hunt, where do I begin? What an adventure! I live in California now, but was born in Texas and my brother still lives there. We decided to help each other out in our states (California was not successful for us). We have a large family and turned this into a family affair. Some put in a lot more effort than others, but the group effort proved successful. I was focused on solving the riddle and my brother was our boots on the ground team member. Day one we spent a lot of time trying to find a New York connection to the state that had to do with a bridge. I remained fixated on bridges throughout and more so footbridges because of the word "walking". At one point during the hunt my brother finally told me, "Enough with the bridges, find something else". That stuck with me though.

After receiving the 1st clue, we were pretty certain it was on the east side of the state. This was great news because my brother let me know that he wasn't driving more than a few hours from where he lived. He was committed, but not totally. The water clue brought me right back to footbridges. We made connections that we thought were good and he spent day two driving and searching near Tomball. After returning home discouraged and annoyed from 8 hours of what turned out to be wasted time, I felt certain I no longer had boots on the ground.

I was talking to my mom about the clues and that we thought is was on the eastern side of the state but we couldn't make any connections to New York, Tom's, or apples; she mentioned that we used to live near Milam Texas and there is a Milam apple, maybe it is there. She didn't know how she knew that but felt it probably had been something her father mentioned as he knew everything plant and tree related in life. We were excited about that news and then went on a search of the town of Milam and came up empty. We then realized there was a county called Milam. Things started falling into place. Two Four Six was no longer confusing to us after researching bridges in Milam county. And then finding one that had been relocated, we felt certain this was the place. When I was talking to my brother and he looked at the map again, he also mentioned Milano's are a cookie. His love of cookies helped too!

We were talking while he was at work and I felt certain we had the place, but it wasn't going to happen that we could get there. I was shocked when he agreed to leave work at 11 pm, told them he was sick and had to go. He then borrowed a phone charger from someone because his phone was nearly dead. He also borrowed gas money from someone because he didn't have that either. He set out on the road and we talked most of the 2 ½ hours it took him to get there. That was an adventure in itself as cell service was not always available and finding the actual location in the middle of the night was also a challenge. When he finally arrived, there were some sketchy people there. After speaking with them and realizing they had nothing to do with the hunt, he decided to start to dig. It was dark, it was freezing, there were sketchy people and the sounds of coyotes around him. His hands were freezing and according to him, snot was totally running down his nose and he only had his sleeve to wipe it on. So gross! He was getting frustrated trying to find it, the digging wasn't paying off, his cell phone wasn't working and then BAM, he found the spot. He was excited he found it. As soon as he got service again, he called me. We truly couldn't believe we had figured it out. Financially it could not have happened at a better time for us. Of course when I told my mom the next morning, she decided it was all because of her and the useless knowledge in her head. (She isn't getting the money!) I was so glad my brother was willing to take another chance on looking after the long day before. All of us are looking forward to next year and doing this all again!

Texas Memories

UTAH

Winner: Heather Wilson

Jones Ironworks Park - Cedar City, UT

Nov 21, 2020 at 12:00 pm - Nov 21, 2020 at 1:13 pm

Riddle:
The man told his oldest son to go grab his metal cane
Mr. Mr. Jones a teacher, liked to walk the little lane
Why he used such a tiny cup to quench his big ole thirst
He wasn't in the woods, so it made no sense at first

Our Utah team, Team Wilson, consists of myself, Heather Wilson, my husband Dale Wilson and my daughter Megan Wilson. Dale and I live in the small town of Grantsville, Utah about 35 miles west of Salt Lake City, where Megan lives. Dale and I have lived in this area for the past 17 years and love the friendliness and quiet of a small town. We have 4 grown kids, 1 granddaughter and 1 grandson on the way. I am a Financial Analyst for a local University, Dale is an independent mobile RV technician, and Megan is a Behavioral Analyst working with autistic children. Ever since I can remember, I have had a love of riddles, mysteries and puzzles. In fact, I am currently working on the world's biggest jigsaw puzzle! Megan knows this, so when she heard about the contest, she told me, and I spent the next 2 ½ months intensely preparing for the hunt.

In preparation, I watched all of the live YouTube videos after each state's hunt, studied the origin and meaning of Utah city names, and any notable places within the cities. Since we live hours away from many locations in the state, I decided to have our team split up to cover more areas. Dale drove south, I went to central Utah, and Megan stayed in the Salt Lake area. My sister Emily, daughter Rebbecca and son Josh were also aware, and willing to go somewhere if needed. On the morning of the hunt, Dale, Megan and I got on a group call and read through the riddle together, throwing out ideas. Immediately I saw little cup and thought Dixie. Also, I initially thought that Mr. Mr. stood for the band, and that a member had the last name George. St. George is known as Utah's Dixie, so initially, that is where we decided to send Dale and he left Cedar City within minutes. On his way out of town, however, I read the word teacher and thought it looked familiar. I looked at my list of cities and saw that Enoch meant teacher, also that the metal in "metal cane" meant Iron, which could mean Iron county. Dale was unsure whether to keep heading to St. George or go to Enoch until Megan found the Iron Works Park in Enoch. We decided it was a better choice than St. George, so Dale took the Enoch exit. As he was looking for the park, Megan found the marker online and said it looked identical to the picture. Then we found the writing on the marker mentioned "Jones". We realized this was it, and after taking a few minutes to direct Dale to the marker, he made it. He found the gravel, started pushing it aside and then shouted "I got it!" This whole process took 15 minutes to solve, 15 minutes to find the marker and 5 minutes to get the necklace. The rest of the day was a mix of unbelief, excitement and joy. We are so grateful to David and Stephanie for making this possible, and letting us be a part of a great adventure!

Utah
Memories

VERMONT

Winner: Kelly Martin

Moxley Covered Bridge - Tunbridge, VT

Oct 24, 2020 at 12:00 pm - Oct 24, 2020 at 1:15 pm

Riddle:
The man stood 10' 6" tall
He was very troubled, and had moxy y'all
On his left his 4 friends grew
It's under a rock you'll start to accrue

In September my husband, Chris showed me the news article about The Gold Ticket scavenger hunt. We decided to get a NH entry. The next day I decided to also buy a Maine and VT entry. Maine's hunt happened and we were not even close to finding it which was okay because we had a great weekend in Maine and still had VT and NH hunts to do.

The week before Vermont's riddle release we started to plan out where we were going to start. We planned to be in Vermont right when the riddle was released. A few days before the release Chris was talking with a friend about going to a covered bridge. Then he told me about it. At that point he started thinking a covered bridge would be a good spot to hide the ticket.

On the release date we drove to Vermont and stopped just over the VT line at Quechee Gorge to wait for the riddle to be released. When the riddle was released Chris read the part that said the man stood 10'6" tall and thought it could be a covered bridge. He googled covered bridges in Vermont which brought up over 100 bridges. Not knowing all the towns in Vermont, Chris then Googled covered bridges in Moxy. Google reveled Moxley Covered Bridge in Chelsea, VT which was 32 min from where we were. We started driving towards there since it was the only lead we had.

As Chris was driving I continued to research. The riddle also said "on his left his 4 friends grew. It also had a picture to show where the ticket was. When I was researching the Moxley Covered bridge I pulled up pictures of the bridge which showed the 4 trees to the left of the bridge. At that point we KNEW we had the right place we just had to be the first ones there. We drove like the wind. Our adrenaline was pumping and every minute felt like 10. When we got there we ran to the trees and moved some rocks. I did not read the note that said it was buried under the rock. We moved several rocks and was heart broken, we thought we were to late. We took some pictures to show we found the location but we were to late. I then went to the car and sat down to try to check the account to see if the ticket had been claimed. We had no service so I was trying several different things. As I was doing that my husband said we should at least try the metal detector. As I looked at my phone my husband went over and swept over the area. He said it beeped and he dug a bit with his fingers. Then a tiny bit of gold showed. He picked it up, turned towards me in the car and threw it up into the air. Then he saw I still had my head down and didn't see anything. He picked up the ticket and came to the car. With my head still down I said "Nothing huh?" He tossed the ticket into my lap. I grabbed it, screamed, jumped out of the car and ran over and jumped into my husbands arms. We ran around screaming for at least 10 minutes. We couldn't believe it. Since we didn't have service we had to drive back towards town to email that we found it. It was at that point I saw the "NOTE" saying it was buried. Not reading the entire riddle almost cost us five thousand dollars.

This experience has been the most exciting experience I have ever had and to do it with my ·husband was the greatest.

Vermont Memories

VIRGINIA I

Winner: Cody & Sandra Parker

AAF Tank Museum - Danville, VA

Oct 2, 2020 at 11:00 am - Oct 6, 2020 at 12:04 pm

Riddle:
I couldn't find a band of gold
as I go to the right of the cross
I tracked my vision to the middle
Find a crack and some rocks, don't piddle.

Clue 1:
He was a famous trumpet man
from out Chicago way.

Clue 2:
Johnny and Dan way back in 97
didn't cost them a dime
but it did, their friend Kevin.

Clue 3:
Tracks with no rail
Hope you get some mail
See exhibit or restore
So so big, you might adore

Clue 4:
The train might have brought you
You're about 12 minutes away
Find another method of transportation
Look in some rocks today

Dear Stephanie and Candyman

Hello everybody we are the Parker family. My wife's name is Sandra, I'm Cody, and our three-year-old is Geppetto. Thank You for taking the time to read our story. Most people in the contest would know us as the first Virginia winners. Then again there's been a lot of debate on that! Though if you could be so kind as to check out our story, I think you'll understand just how everything unfolded that brought us to the gold ticket in Virginia. To add just a little bit more about us, I'm a CDL bus driver, and my wife is a stay-at-home mom. She is very creative, and loves all forms of art. I myself have my own form of art, which is coming up with ideas for inventions. Our son Geppetto is full of joy, and loves learning anything and everything.

Our journey to The Gold Ticket started with none other than my wife Sandra. She has had a long-time fascination with Charlie and the chocolate factory. She participated in many different candy company games in the past, where they hid gold tickets in chocolate. So, when she heard in the news that the Candyman and Stephanie were hosting a real-life gold ticket scavenger hunt, we were in. We bought our ticket, and eagerly awaited a month for our state to go live.

We were super excited as the riddle was about to be released, and dove head in trying to find a thread to pull. We researched from home anything we could think of, from giant crosses, to the pyrite belt here in Virginia. Then my wife was able to put together quite a few coincidences that seemed to lead us to Bristol Virginia, right along the Tennessee border. So, we all hopped in the car and headed that way. It is a bit of a stretch for us at 3 hours and 45 minutes down the Shenandoah Valley. We searched high and low around everything we could think of, but since the ticket wasn't there, we ended up heading home, with one long day under our belt.

With the release of the first Hint, that day ended up being an extensive research day, literally morning to night. We tried everything we could think of to crack Stephanie's code, but we weren't quite sure what direction to go. Once again, we started another long research day, then in the evening we ended up having a bit of a family emergency. Everybody's okay, but we did have to go to the ER for about four hours, (None Corona Virus Related). We thought for sure our scavenger hunt was over.

When the next day rolled around, we had our minds on life stuff. I had to pick up a prescription at Walmart, and I decided to grab a couple key groceries for the month. I had just bought 60 eggs, over 10 lb. of burger, and a few jugs of milk. Pretty much all the perishable stuff. Low and behold, my phone dings with the next Hint. Immediately this clue seemed to open up a bunch of doors for us on as to where the ticket could be. My wife ironically had another very coincidental lead in Richmond. After some pretty excited deep deliberation, we decided that I could at least drive out there and check. It was best for my wife and my son to stay home, since this was just going to be a quick back and forth to Richmond.

I got to the location at the Richmond Science Center, and searched thoroughly every place I could look. With no luck, I started some more research in the car, and so did my wife Sandra at home. We realized based upon multiple points in the riddle that the same things that sent us to the Richmond Science Center, also correlated with the Danville Science Center. Again, me being a bus driver, I tend to pull some long miles on the road, so it wasn't that big a deal for me to head to Danville from Richmond. As I drove, my wife continued to do research, and found the small crossroad area known as Ringgold. Plus, there is a hiking trail, called The Ringgold Rail Trail, that follows along an old railroad track. There's even a red caboose parked at the one end of the trail, a post office, and a church. If you read through the riddle, I think you could see why we thought it could be there.

As I was getting close to Danville, we realize that this might actually fit better than even the Danville Science Center. So here I am going off into the deep deep woods to checked all the different the trailheads to this place. My phone GPS almost completely stopped working, so it was quite complicated figuring out where to go. I looked under rocks, in the dirt, and even under a porta potty with no luck, don't piddle...hahaha. With no luck there, I decided to roll into Danville and give my luck checking out the areas that we had thought near The Crossing, and the Danville Science Center. By the time I had done all this driving and searching, it actually started to get dark on me, so there was only limited searching I could even do. We had heard a handful of other people had also decided to go there too, with no luck.

Not to mention I had to stop and buy a cooler, and a bunch of ice, just to try to keep all of my groceries that I forgot to take out of the car, cold. Nothing like having a whole bunch of perishables with you on a scavenger hunt. After checking a few more places, plus some parks in the area I pulled into a rest area right near the Virginia line off of 29. Talking with my wife we really felt like we were so close. It just had to be somewhere down here, we thought. So, we came to the conclusion that I would just sleep in the car right there, ruff it overnight, and hold out for the next hint. We had all our stuff packed for scavenger hunting still in the car, so I had some clothes, a sleeping bag, and some snacks. Researching on the phone, and talking with my wife late into the night was the end of our day four, and a memory I'll never forget.

Day Five, The Day of The Gold 10/06/2020

With the coldness that came in around Dawn, plus the excitement of the day's possibilities, I was awake early. In just only a few more short hours, we knew we could have the clue that brings us to the gold. We had a couple more possibilities to check now that it was light. Plus, I knew I needed to get some more ice to take care of the perishables. I ended up at Walmart, and got some the supplies, then went back to researching. I was looking over the list that we had come up with, of all the possible places we thought it could be.

It so funny, but at 8:17am that morning, I sent my wife an email telling her to re-check out more details about the AAF Tank Museum. She had added it to our list days ago. It did seem to fit with different parts of the riddle, but we were still unsure. I saved the tank museum in my GPS, so I could reference it quickly if the next Hint pointed to it. I realize now that I was only about eight minutes away from the Museum at that time. We still felt like our best location was the Danville science Center, so that's where I headed back to.

The Release of The Final Hint

Then came The Final Hint. There were so many parts in that hint that lined right up with the Tank Museum. On top of that, I checked my GPS almost immediately, and it said that I was 12 minutes away from the tank museum. I kicked it in gear, and headed that way. I pulled into the tank museum at 11:12am, right as one other couple was getting out of their car. Immediately seeing the tank and at least two or three large planters filled with rocks and signs. I knew that if the gold ticket was here, that it was probably in one of those planners with the rocks. I wanted to do my part to social distance, so I went to the rock planner where the other couple wasn't. I tried to scoop one direction with the stones, and then scoop the stones back to where they had been with the next scoop. I'm a fairly logical person, so I decided on a systematic approach to carefully go around the whole edge of each rock, railroad tie planter. I'm pretty tall too, so I was able to reach to the middle, and even check around the stones at the base of the sign. Then one of the other hunters came over and started looking in the same planter. I felt like I had checked that planner quite well, so I moved on to the next. I had no luck there either.

So, I decided to head up to the third one, which was over near the door. There was a very nice girl who had been looking, and I didn't want to get in her way, so I tried to stay on the opposite side of the planter as she was looking. I used my systematic scooping to check around the edge. I started with the side closest to the building, and then the part that would be considered the back of the planner.

Then I came up the other side. I also was reaching into the middle some to check around the base of the information stone that was there. I was starting my approach to do the front, now that the girl had moved away, and then that's when it happened. A very strong-spoken individual came outside, wearing tan camo, and with a very commanding tone announced "IF ANYBODY DAMAGES ANYTHING, THEY WILL BE HELD RESPONSIBLE".

Now I am paraphrasing a little bit, but that has to be mighty close to the exact words he used. Also, he pretty much insisted that anybody anywhere remotely inside the planners need to get out, and everybody had to stop digging. I realize things had gotten quite busy there, with the sheer number of people that had been pouring in. As I looked up, I saw people walking everywhere. Some along the edge of the building, others by the tank, and the planters. Nothing seemed damaged, but stones were ruffled in different places.

I'm sure it probably looked very odd to the employees, to look out their window and randomly see all these people outside searching. My wife had a funny thought, when I told her about it later on the phone.

She thought that they might have thought, it was a rock eating zombie attack! So here I am apparently standing only like an arm's stretch away from where the golden ticket is hidden, with full intentions of systematically checking that exact side of the planter next. Then again, at the time I didn't know that it was there, but where else could it be. This was the last main planter to check, and that was the only side I hadn't checked yet. Since we were told to stop, I wasn't sure what to do. I wanted to finish looking, I planned on looking, but I had to walk away. I thought well maybe I can just visually look for it, without touching anything. I walked back over to the tank, and I looked there for a minute.

Then I heard the gentleman say something else. He had been frantically trying to prevent the cars from pulling in, since it was one car after another. I heard him say "if you damage anything, I'm going to call the cops", and then immediately say, "you know what, I should just call the cops right now". I knew at that point that something had to be done to de-escalate the excitement. I also knew that I could no longer look the way that I needed to find a ticket.

I was thinking about how our whole family had so fun researching, and going on this adventure. Even though my wife and son had to stay home for the second leg of it, we had communicated almost constantly on the phone, so they were with me. I didn't want this contest to leave a sour taste in anybody's mouth. I figured I should contact Stephanie and David; they would know what to do. The guy there really wanted everybody to clear out, so I told him I was leaving as I got in my car, and I drove across the street and parked. There I emailed Stephanie and David, and told them what was going on. I mention to them that the cops were on their way, and that they needed to address all the treasure hunters before things got out of hand.

I told them I don't know what to do, I can't search anymore. Also, that I had been so excited to be one of the first people there. Everything in the riddle leads both me and my wife to that being the right place. With a sad feeling, I knew it was time to go, so I pulled out of there. I wasn't even a few miles down the road when my wife called me and told me "guess what Cody, they just announced you as the winner." She also told me that they wanted me to call in. I had my headset on, which allows me to drive and talk, but I wanted to pull over. Then we had to play the wrong phone number game apparently. I tried three or four times to call them with the wrong phone number.

I even had my wife looking up the right one, and somehow got Chuck-E-Cheese. I was finally able to get through, and it was such an honor to talk with Stephanie and David. Then again, I've never talked to anybody famous before, so I was a little amped from everything. I explained to them just how tricky the situation had gotten there. I knew that I didn't break anything, but the stones were ruffled pretty good.

I started thinking that I had my landscaping gloves in the back, so I offered to David that I could go back to the tank museum, and see if I could help straighten out the stones. David and Stephanie asked me, to offer them a donation of $500 to make up for the trouble, on their behalf. I thought that was a really kind of a generous offer, since as far as I had seen, nothing but the stones had been ruffled.

I went back to where they had a little barricade up by the entrance. The individual's there were dealing with other treasure hunters coming to search. It was clear at this point that they didn't want any more treasure hunters coming on the property. I had to announce to them that I had David on the phone, and that I was here to help and that he wants to make things right with the donation. That seemed to calm things down a little bit. They move the barricade and had me pull back in. Right about that same time is when an officer pulled up. I only had a short chance to talk with the employees of the museum, since they needed to go talk with the officer. I waited off to the side for about 20 minutes. When the officer was leaving, I finally got a chance to talk to them again. I gave them David's information to call, and that he is willing to make a donation of $500. I also offered to help to straighten up the area, by smoothing out the stones.

They didn't want any help, they just wanted everything left the way it was. We started talking about what the contest was about. How there was a gold ticket hidden somewhere? Earlier while I had been waiting, Stephanie emailed me. She thought it would be good to retrieve the gold ticket, since I was there. She had sent me a picture of the ticket's hiding spot. I instantly knew right where that was, even though the picture was a very close up shot. That was the center edge of the planter that I was literally checking when the man came out yelling. Right smack in the middle of the front side of the planter. So now here I am talking with that same strong presence individual. When he realized I knew where the ticket was, he demanded that I show him. I said "it would be good for us to get the ticket, because I wanted it as a keepsake". I guess he was still a little upset, because he said

"you're going to get it right now, and you're going to give it to me, because I'm going to rip it up".

I guess he didn't know that it was a metal tag. I didn't want to argue, or make anything worse, so I went over to the spot and started looking. It was right where Stephanie had said, but I did have to look for a good 30 seconds or so. Right as the man was losing patience, and told me that's enough and to stop, I had gotten a glimmer of the gold chain. I pulled it out of the stones. I know he wanted it but I just had to take a few seconds to hold it, and look at it. It was a real humbling experience to just hold the thing after thinking about it so much over the last month. The gentleman pretty much put out his hand, I knew I had to hand it over. As we're both walking back up towards the entrance, some of the other treasure hunters across the road saw that we had pulled something out of the stones.

They were just wanting some verification that the ticket was 100% there, and that the hunt was officially over. They had yelled for us to swing the gold chain around overhead. At the time they didn't realize that this gentleman holding it was an employee of the tank museum, and still sort of unhappy with the situation. I tried to calm them down, by telling them that the contest is over, and that we just need to let it go. I mean I just had to give up the Gold Ticket myself. They were really wanting to see it, so they were pushing a bit. I headed to my vehicle, so I never saw whether the gentleman in the camo swung the chain or not. They didn't want any help fixing any of the stones, they just told me to go ahead and go. As I was pulling out there, I saw another trooper pulling in. So, in my opinion it was time to go.

Virginia I
Memories

VIRGINIA II

Winner: Bobby Dunbar

Fenwick Mines - New Castle, VA

Oct 22, 2020 at 11:00 am - Oct 22, 2020 at 7:19 pm

Riddle:
A famous treasure guy in Santa Fe was he
He needed a candle burnt at both ends while drinking tea
Go look behind and you will surely find
A necklace that means so much to me

Our team name was Dunbar Treasure Hunting Adventurers
It was
Me: Bobby Dunbar (AKA) Bobby D
Robert Dunbar: My Dad
Goldie Dunbar: My Mom
Roberta Jo Fleshman: My Sister

We did the first West Virginia hunt, the Kentucky Hunt, (knew the location but it was solved while we were on our way there)

The Virgina Re-Do (The one we WON!) and the West Virginia Re-do, (Also found while we were on our way to the location).

We have done many treasure hunts in the past, mostly the team was just Me, My Dad and Mom, we won 2 previous radio treasure hunts from J104.5 FM (Bluefield) $10,000 Treasure Hunt. It was a lot of fun, but after we won the contest in 2002 and 2003 back to back, they quit doing the hunt. I have won several other small treasure hunts, and the K92.3 FM Secret Sound contest many times, and "helped" my family members win as well. All total we won the secret sound 11 or 12 times. I also did a secret sound from North Carolina and won over $11,000 in that contest. I look forward to the Factory Hunt, and the next round of Gold Ticket Hunts and I want to thank David, Stephanie, Mindy, and EVERYONE involved in these hunts, it was a blast!

WASHINGTON

9/11 Memorial - Kennewick, WA

Oct 24, 2020 at 1:00 pm - Oct 24, 2020 at 7:19 pm

Riddle:
The CooCoo Clock Xerus Could Vanish
Round and round the night visions I banish
Look up and remember them and that day
in a bush not far away is your play

Our team consisted of Becky, Patrick and myself. Becky is the Brainiac who solved the riddle enough for us to know where the ticket may be. We were all thinking about the riddle and were getting stumped, but she was able to get it figured out and we were on our way. It was so exciting to see the gold necklace and realize that we had solved the riddle. This was such a fun experience and just what 2020 needed. Thank you all so much!

WEST VIRGINIA

Winner: Zane Cunningham, Vincent DeMarco, Reagan Flaherty

John Forbes Nash Memorial - Bluefield, WV

Oct 9, 2020 at 11:00 am - Oct 13, 2020 at 8:00 am

Riddle:
They told us they're with us in strange ways you see
They told us to count and play together with me
I drive over there, up the street and even down
I know they are with me, when I play round and round

Clue 1:
Balance is what we all need in life.
Deciding who wins you wouldn't ask the wife.

Clue 2:
A black bird in the wild loves shiny things
He'll pick a rock that holds some bling
hidden in a small little shrub on the ground
Look for the words so that it can be found

Clue 3:
Don't make me sad in the big open space
Shuffle to the right when you see his face
A big rock is in front a little to the right
Enjoy your find it's out of sight.

My mom and I were looking for The Gold Ticket for about a week. My mom lives in Bluefield. After being stumped on the riddle were able to piece together where we thought the gold necklace was located. The clue about it being hidden in a little shrub on the ground, look for the words so it can be found gave us a great idea to where it can be located, and we headed to where we thought the spot was. We found the necklace in a fake rock, and what helped us to search the spot is it had been freshly mulched and we remember seeing the rock and thinking it was so out of place. This was such an awesome treasure hunt and we really enjoyed this! Looking forward to what next hunt brings!

~Zane

I had completed the Virginia hunt (the first one) with my husband. I went down the wrong rabbit hole and refused to look up. I missed obvious clues and the dog tags were found an hour from my home, while I went to the wrong location 4 times, that was 3 hours away.

I was determined to not make the same mistake during the WV hunt. I knew I had to be open minded and keep coming back to the riddle, but use the clues to help with the riddle, not the other way around.

I had set up to spend the weekend with a fellow "retired soccer mom" - our kids no longer play soccer. Her and I became close over the years as we both lost our best friends in different incidents. My best friend's name was Beth and this friend happens to also be a Beth. Her best friend that she lost was a friend of mine, named Kim.

We built a small team with several friends and family members on it. They were my mother and three good friends. Beth and I would be behind the wheel and they would research from home. We packed preparing for the weekend.

Day 1 - a Friday - the riddle was released. It didn't make sense to either of us. We planned to hit the road early on Day 2

Day 2 - Saturday. We immediately made a bee line for Pearl Buck's childhood home. "The Wife" directed us towards a Nobel Prize Winner. We also saw many beautiful things. We saw Patch Adams Hospital in the middle of no where, WV. We went to Charleston and stayed the night.

Day 3 - Sunday. We went to Glenville. We had totally forgot the Nobel Prize winner and thought maybe there was a Square Dancing connection. There wasn't. We then went back to Charleston, WV, looked some, then headed back to VA.

Day 4 - Monday. When the clue came out Monday morning, I wanted to be in WV for the release time. I was late. This time I had my mother in the car with me. We crossed into WV near Lewisburg and quickly realized we needed to be in Bluefield. At this point John Nash kept crossing our minds. We realized he checked off a lot of the boxes. We could not locate anything other than a street marker, that marked his family home. We spent some time at the Bluefield Post Office due to the black birds (the postal emblem, bird and there was a black one on the railing). By 5:45pm, we moved along the road in this area. We went to a an old psychiatric hospital that was a block or so down the same road.

By this time - 6ish, my mother is very upset with me as the trip was much longer than she agreed to. She was hungry and there was a Little Caesars nearby. While she was inside, I kept googling trying to find something to do with Nash, I kept coming up short. then in Google Maps, I saw this random small park looking place, and convinced her to stop there with me on our way out of town (maybe 6:15ish).

We stopped there. I parked directly next to two black iron eagles. I was like "no way" then I jumped out of the car, very excited....

Around the corner of this small park, I found THE ROCK!!! the rock that had John Nash on it. I was skipping, jumping, O'My God, this is it, this is it!!! we looked everywhere. I looked under the bushes, which there were only two small ones in the recently manicured park and both easy to look under and around. (I have pictures). Then we looked in the large bushes, but only found trash. Then we looked everywhere, we did not leave a place untouched, even the trash cans, which were small pebbles glued to a bin. I sent two emails during this time to the main email address. Then my phone died as I was also using the flashlight on it. During this search, we found one larger rock, maybe two hand sized. It was not a fake rock, it had some yellow paint on it, but nothing else. By this time, my mother is yelling at me. She is so ready to go. I finally was like, Okay.

The whole way home, I could not shake the idea that I was definitely in the right spot and it was gone... the dog tags were gone.

Day 5 - Tuesday. I reviewed everything, couldn't sleep. I sent an email with lots of detail to David and Stephanie around 4am. David quickly emailed me back. We exchanged a couple emails. He asked me to call him. by the time, my husband is just stepping out of the shower. David was asking me if I could go back to the park and confirm it was really gone. It was over 2 hours from home. Yes, of course I will go back. I told my husband he needed to take the day off and go with me. He was like, yeah right. I watched you as you were so WRONG in VA, I don't believe you. I pointed to the phone and said I am talking to David. I was right, I was right.

Jeremiah took the day off and drove me... I am so grateful as I had driven over 1500 miles that weekend. We went back to Chicory Square and I called David and Stephanie. The rock was definitely not there. I spoke to them while I searched. It was raining, but I didn't care.

I was determined to be a co-winner with another gentleman.

It was so fun and exhilarating and exactly what I needed. Both my husband and I are Veterans. He was in the Army and I was in the USCG. He is now fighting lymphoma due to exposure to the Burn Pits. Our last year has been a little yuckie due to this and then of course Covid. This is definitely one of the highlights of my year.

~Reagan

Our team consisted of my wife, Tiffany; my dad, John; my mom, Roberta; my sister, MaryJo; my cousin, Mary Ann; my friend, Christie; and me, Vincent. Before the hunt, we all decided to be in different parts of the state. My wife and I were stationed in the southern part of the state, where we stayed in various hotel rooms over 4 days. Throughout the 4 days, we knew that we were in the correct part of the state, but we just couldn't seem to find the necklace. On the first day, which was Friday, the part of that riddle that read "they're with us in strange ways" made us think of Lake Shawnee Abandoned Amusement Park in Mercer County, so my wife and I went there first and had no luck. On Saturday, the hint mentioned "Balance", so we headed to the Mercer County Courthouse, but again had no luck!

On Sunday, the hint talked about "A black bird", so we headed to Snowshoe because there is a golf course there called The Raven. The hint on Monday gave us all the answers we needed. The hint said, "Don't make me sad in the big open space," which meant Blue for sad and Field for big open space. After doing a little more research about Bluefield, we found out that John Forbes Nash is from Bluefield, and all the clues were about him. Because of that, we headed straight for the John Forbes Nash Memorial in Bluefield, WV.

However, we hunted around the memorial for hours with no luck. After reading and re-reading the riddle and hints, I knew that there was no way that it couldn't be there, so I ended up submitting that I didn't believe the gold necklace was actually at the location. I was called the next day that that was the actual location and the place was recently landscaped. A week later, a man finally came forward and said he had found the gold necklace before the hunt even started.

~Vincent

WEST VIRGINIA II

Winner: Larry Stegman

Hometown Community Park - Hometown, WV

Nov 4, 2020 at 4:00 pm - Nov 4, 2020 at 10:16 pm

Riddle:
You don't need to leave your village to find me
Even though you'll be outside to find thee
Not sure how far you'll need to drive
It's out there under the first archive

My team is made up of several people. On the ground and traveling with me in West Virginia were my long-time friend Brenna, her mother Sandy and her two children; Jacob who is 9 and Isaac who is 7. Jacob and Isaac are my God-children. I am their primary care-giver after mom and dad. Also on my team is my daughter, Robyn, who is leading the Delaware search. I hold four tickets: Michigan, Indiana, Delaware and West Virginia. Rounding out our team I have a few friends who provide an extra set of eyes and assistance in the arm-chair part of the search.

I live in Michigan and my first ticket was my home state. I quickly picked up Indiana, the state where I was born, and added West Virginia to my collection to get a little practice at the hunt before it came to Michigan. I later added Delaware for Robyn, who lives in Baltimore, Maryland after having a great time on the original West Virginia hunt.

Since the original West Virginia hunt was my trial run, and it involved 6 hours of driving each way just to get to the state, I was alone on the ground. I drove down to West Virginia the night before the riddle dropped and set up a war room in a hotel room in Williamston, WV. Within an hour of receiving the riddle I was headed to Grafton, the home of mother's day. It was the first of two trips there. Over the course of the next few days I would search Charleston, including two visits to a Chuck Yeager monument in the form of a rocket ship. I crossed the entire state multiple times including stops in Morgantown, Sutton and even Odd. On the day it was found, I was on the ground in Bluefield having searched multiple solves in the area. Although I was within two blocks, I did not make it to the correct park that day.

For the West Virginia redo, I did a lot of research and determined that Charleston was the best starting location. My expectation was that the necklace would be found not far from I-64 and this gave us a central starting point. We arrived in Charleston late the night before the riddle dropped and setup in a hotel suite on the south side of town. The morning of the riddle drop we spent exploring Kanawha State Forest. When the riddle dropped, we were poised and ready to begin research. Everyone was ready to head out as soon as we had a good solve.

The riddle led us to search historical libraries and archives initially looking for something we could match up with the rest of the clue. The picture was a key box to tick, when we found a likely location we would check for a similar structure, looking at the pattern of brickwork. In addition to the particular style of brickwork I identified two key features; The pedestal was 4 bricks wide and had one dark brick on the left end of the third row up. We bounced around searching for 'villages' and briefly looking at golf courses (drive) before decided to look for monuments and sign pedestals constructed from bricks. After some exhaustive searching, we came across the pedestal for Hometown. The brickwork style matched very well and the name, Hometown, sealed it. This matched up perfectly with the first line of the riddle. Having found a likely solve, we zoomed in on the spot using Google earth.

The pedestal we could see matched the brickwork extremely well, but it was only 3 bricks across and did not have the dark brick. Looking again at the name Hometown and the style of the brick, it was too good to pass up. At this point it was after 10pm, but the solve was only 43 minutes from our hotel. We decided to pile into the car and have a look. The drive there was an adventure in itself culminating with the arrival at the spot. It was quite a way from the highway or any major towns and pitch black. We poured out of the car and unloaded multiple flashlights and a garden trowel. While everyone else examined the pedestal and found a spot which appeared to match, I fumbled for my phone to match the picture. I was thrilled to find that side of the pillar not visible on Google-earth was 4 bricks wide and had the exact dark brick we had identified. By this time digging was underway. It seemed like we dug for a while before we saw the glint of the necklace. Shouting and hugs ensued as we pulled it from the ground.

We took the time to put the area as we found it before I shakily took a picture to send to Submit.

West Virginia II
Memories

WISCONSIN

Winner: Joshua McDonnell

John and Emma Smrekar Memorial Fountain - Black River Falls, WI

Nov 7, 2020 at 11:00 am - Nov 8, 2020 at 11:23 am

Riddle:
Don't go in the water as it's too dark to see
look on the ground and you'll find me
I'm under some rocks, but don't climb at all
I have fed the needy and that's why I won't fall

Clue 1:
The forest is near the city I am in
You'll need to widen your circle to win
The wheat, the oats they might come here
Don't forget the berries, I'm no Shakespeare

Our team was a husband and wife team, Nicole and Josh McDonnell and we are from Black Earth, WI and our family is us and two dogs. We learned about the hunt through a friend on Facebook who thought this seemed like something we would be into and she was correct. What got us most excited about the whole thing was the adventure of solving a riddle while exploring the state with a hope that it would be something off the beaten path and somewhere we had not explored yet. One of our hobbies since moving here in 2014 is to take off on a side road and just drive to see where we go and yet throughout our drives we had never really explored cranberry country.

Our search story.

We packed some road snacks and we gassed up the truck the night before. The morning of the riddle, five minutes before the riddle was released, we hopped in the truck and waited, phones in hand. The first line of the riddle "Don't go in the water as it's too dark to see" resulted in us just searching for Dark Lake and there was one up north but it was too far for us to travel to so we then looked up mud lake thinking maybe it's about visibility. Unfortunately, there are 100+ "Mud Lakes" in Wisconsin one was in south Madison but did not look to have anything around it. Then we threw "Black Lake Wisconsin" into google and it spit back "Black River." We are both from the Mississippi valley, so the rock type in the picture seemed familiar so it clicked. That was in our two hour drive search window so off we went.

On our way up we took pictures of bluff formations and the scenery and once we got to Black River Falls we could tell we were not the first. The crowds were small at the riverfront initially. By the time we gave up on the river having not found that blueish/green plastic piece in the picture we stopped at the bridge downtown. On the wall of a corner shop there is a quote from Mother Theresa. That set in for us that we must be in the right place so we spent until sunset combing creek paths throughout town while occasionally stopping by various landmarks, like giant metal moose or deer. There were hundreds of people in a town of 4000 people. There was so much energy throughout the day from everyone.

While we headed home we thought for sure it had to be in Black River Falls so planned on getting up early so we could be back in town right at second riddle drop. Additionally, Nicole had to work in the afternoon on Sunday, so we knew we had to be back by 2:00 which would give us about two hours of time searching Black River Falls in the morning.   Reflecting back, three key moments caused us to be at the exact right spot when the riddle hit. Key moment 1) tacos for dinner on our way out of town.   Key moment 2) Once home we were exhausted and did not remember to refill gas. Key moment 3) We went to bed and forgot to set the alarm.

Our dogs woke us wanting to go outside and we noticed we had slept in so instead of an hour to get ready before leaving we had 30 minutes! Once ready at 7:50 (instead of the originally planned 7:30) we hopped in the truck and took off. I looked at the gas tank and saw there was no way we would make it there with what we had so we stopped in Sauk City to fill up on gas. It was another 10 minutes set back. Now our ETA was going to be in Black River Falls right at 10am when the clue dropped instead of slightly before.   But we pressed on. The next hour or so was an easy drive until uh oh... taco tummy rumbles... needed to stop off at the next gas station. Pulled over to the Home Front Cafe in Camp Douglas with the additional plan of getting Quiznos as well. Unfortunately at the time, fortunately for this story, the Quiznos was closed so we hopped back on the road. ETA 10:15 for Black River Falls.

The clue was released just north of the Three Bears Resort at the Warrens exit. As Nicole read the clue aloud, she started researching mills in Black River Falls based around the clue "The wheat, the oats they might come here" but at that moment I saw and read allowed the road sign "Exit 128, O Millston" and she hit my arm saying "You'll need to widen your circle to win." The exit was onto County Road O.   So at 10:03AM we got off the highway to the town that likely should not have even had an exit for it and started driving around town.   We drove to the park just repeating the two riddles and saw that blueish/green box and a sign saying "Do Not Climb On Rocks" and Nicole yelled "I'm under some rocks, but don't climb at all" from the riddle.   Nicole almost jumped out of the truck before it stopped and we ran over. She flipped a rock or two next to the box and I pulled up the picture to find a matching rock. It was 10:07AM and we started thinking there was no way someone got here before us so I walked to the side of the blueish/green box and tried to match the rocks that Nicole had already flipped. No luck... something was off. The picture showed a cable but there was no cable. But there in the picture was a weed! That weed matched a weed behind the box! I quickly moved a few rocks out of the way and pulled out the gold ticket under just a bit of dirt. It was 10:08AM and we were ecstatic. I was shaking from the adrenaline and Nicole was yelling "we need to get out of here" but I knew we needed to document. As she took pictures, my hand was shaking as I typed the email and kept asking her to confirm that I typed the gold ticket number right. We ran back to the truck at 10:12AM and hit send on the email "Wisconsin Found!" We then drove to TKs 400 Club lot which overlooks the park and waited.

In the three minutes between us sending the email and the first response, 4 vehicles arrived the first at 10:14 and the guy jumped out of his moving truck and ran to the area just as we had. During the interview more and more people were showing up until there were about 20 standing around.   Had we not; overslept, forgotten to gas up the truck, gotten taco tummy rumbles, we would have been in Black River Falls, about 14 minutes North of Millston with the crowd that showed up 10:14. Had Quiznos been open, and we got sandwiches, we would have been about 14 minutes south of the Millston exit and likely would have turned off at Warrens.   It turns out what we thought were answers to the riddle (the Mother Theresa quote and the Highway O were just circumstantial.

The Candyman said it perfectly in our interview "There's a lot of skill in this, but there's a little bit of luck that you were right there." Our treasure hunt embodied that quote and we had an absolute blast. Thank you for the adventure!

We were so thrilled to be a part of this treasure hunt, we are from Black Earth, WI. We were about an hour away from where we had found The Gold Ticket in Black River Falls. We used the part in the riddle about feeding the needy to find some details on people that had helped feed the homeless, and deciphering the riddle further had led us to Black River Falls. When we arrived we did see other searchers looking for the necklace. We knew we weren't the only ones that had figured out the riddle. Once we were able to locate the necklace we did take off quickly. It was so fun to be able to win something and have the best time doing it. We found out about the hunt on Facebook and thought this would be an interesting event to do. Never looked back, and now we are looking forward to future hunts!

WYOMING

Winner: Jessica Lippincott

Worland Sugar Factory - Worland, WY

Oct 29, 2020 at 3:00 pm - Oct 29, 2020 at 7:23 pm

Riddle:
This town is such a treat and really really sweet
Daddy came upon it and was shy until you'd meet
The necklace is placed "low", a bit lower than your feet
Enjoy this veggie now, you'll really want to eat

David had called us when all 8 of us were on the road. We had heard about The Gold Ticket in August and purchased our ticket in Sep. We found our Gold Ticket in Worland, Wyoming! We got the riddle at 1PM and got to work right away. I started thinking about sweets and sugar, we even searched in Google sugar factory in Wyoming. This is in combination with going through some of the towns, we were able to narrow it down to Worland. We found the original town site and the sugar cane factory marker and knew this is where it was. This was such an awesome experience and we hope to do it again very soon!

A Note from

David & Stephanie

I have always had a fascination with treasure. I loved to metal detect. I loved to make treasure hunts to find gifts for my kids. Every year our local newspaper would have a treasure hunt and I couldn't wait to give it a try. In 2011 I was ready to put on my own treasure hunt and decided to look to see if anyone had done something like that when I came across a man who said he hid a treasure in the mountains North of Santa Fe worth millions. I put down my own treasure hunting idea and took off for Colorado. I spent 10 years getting to know this man and searched more places than seems possible when looking back. It later appeared to me that it might not have been what it appeared to be, I could either be sad about all the time and money I lost chasing or I could turn it into a positive and put on a treasure hunt that would be fair and transparent.

Together David and I would come together with our dreams and combine them and create the most wonderful experience of our lives called The Gold Ticket Treasure Hunt. The first of hopefully many Candyman Treasure Hunts.

In 2018 we filed a treasure hunting patent and in 2019 we started a couple online treasure hunting games of skill. In 2020 we were finally ready to run our first Boots on The Ground Treasure Hunt. We had planned to start with only 9 states, but David spoke to a friend of his at the Associated Press who was willing to write up a story about our great Gold Ticket Treasure Hunt, but said that it would be best to run the story after we opened it up for all the states since their coverage is nationwide. That's when we took the crazy leap. We had our website www.TheGoldTicket.com completed and opened it up for all 50 states figuring that we probably would lose a bunch of money, but we knew no matter what happened that we'd have the time of our lives.

About two days after opening up our website, the news picked up our story and it went viral. People we hadn't spoken to in years contacted us asking was that really you on the Nightly News? Our treasure hunt story was on all over social media, and all the networks picked it up.

From David regarding Jelly Belly® jelly beans......

Within a few days I learned that Jelly Belly® jelly beans had come out with a press release that stated the following....

"David Klein, the sponsor of the "treasure hunt" contest gaining attention within the media this weekend, is not associated with Jelly Belly Candy Company, its brands, or products. In 1976, Mr. Klein, an independent third party, came up with the name "Jelly Belly" and other novel marketing ideas. Jelly Belly Candy Company has not had a relationship with Mr. Klein since 1980 when it acquired the trademark."

I'd like to say a few things about this statement. First of all, I will and always have been associated with Jelly Belly as I created the product, and founded my own company called Jelly Belly Company. Proof is in the check below as well as many other documents I can provide. From the year 1976-1980 I not only created the product and the concept of unique flavors, but I single-handedly made the product a huge success by being on nationwide TV, in nationwide print magazines, and newspapers. My product became an overnight success and was requested from nationwide high end retail locations like Marshall Fields in Chicago.

For those who are not familiar with my documentary called Candyman The David Klein Story, I welcome you to view it. It briefly describes how my contract manufacturer The Herman Goelitz Company(Now Jelly Belly Candy Company) told me they were coming to town to buy my trademark and were not leaving until they did. The documentary doesn't get into the details I wish it had, but I will do that here. I was told that if I did not sell my trademark, that they would cut off my supply and rename my product and they had a list of my customers to sell to. At that time there were very few candy companies that would be able to replicate my jelly bean.

So my choice was simple. Take their offer or lose everything I had worked to build up. The offer in dollars, was the same amount I was already earning with my product. They got what they wanted and they have been trying to write me out of the history ever since. If you ask Google who invented Jelly Belly® jelly beans, it will tell you the founder of their company who wasn't even alive at that time. If you try to get press, you are told you aren't allowed to say you are the founder, because they have contacted the press to dispute what I say.

The last thing I'd like to correct in their statement, is that they said they have had nothing to do with me since 1980. This is not true, since the last check didn't arrive till 2000.

In closing....

I've gotten to a point in my life, that I know I can't dwell on what happened even though I feel I was cheated. I try to think about the jobs my product created for so many good people. I was on the Mike Douglas Show in 1977 and they flew me 1st class to Philadelphia to tape the show. They picked me up in a limousine the day of the show, and brought me to Westinghouse Network Studio. The co-host that week was Anthony Newley who happened to be the co composer of the hit song Candyman.

As I was running down the aisle to go on the stage he sang the song Candyman to me. It was at that precise moment that I decided some day I wanted to give away one of my candy factories to a complete stranger. This thought has been on my bucket list ever since then and I'm very happy that I'm able to do this at this point of my life.

I try to think about all the celebrations and good times my creation was involved in for people across the world. It doesn't mean that I don't sometimes get into that place that remembers those feelings though. I know many people can relate to that. I now get to be a part of something new and exciting and feel the love from others who see the type of person I am. I love to give and make people happy. We are building a community of like minded people. These friends have become our family.

Riddles & Solutions (State wise)

Alabama:

Riddle:
Jen wasn't in Virginia when she brought flowers to her Mom
The threshold they were crossing was not very calm
paint showed the history and sound came from near
Wish I could say I'm sorry, even though I wasn't even there.

Riddle Solution:
Jen (Jennifer A(n)niston.
Virginia (Boynton vs Virginia)
Flowers to mom (Mother's Day)
Threshold (that's where it's hidden by the mural where a door is)
not calm (they were taking a stand)
paint and sound (there's a painting of the bus and a recording nearby)

Alaska:

Riddle:
Mr. John met Mr. Stewart at Mr. Tylers
Imagine taking the train downtown and you'll be a smiler
Go to Philadelphia and do what it takes
To go to the Arctic and buy a Kodiak and Shake!

Clue 1:
Yesterday's riddle was on the radio so loud
I loved it so much my head was in a cloud
With my arms stretched out so wide
A bird landed on them with pride

Clue 2:
If you thought Elton you were on the right track.
The first riddle was all about music, it's fact.
What genre is here and here to stay
Behind the tree and on the ground it lay
P.S. We told Karen where he is.

Riddle Solution:
Elton, Stewart, Tyler (Elton John, Rod Stewart, Steven Tyler)
Train downtown (song by Rod Stewart called Downtown Train)
what it takes (Aerosmith)
Philadelphia (Elton John)
Shake! (Rod Stewart)
Clue 1: (Think of music)(head in cloud because the head on the statue is so big)
Clue 2: (genre-ROCK)(Karen=Cairn)

Arizona

Riddle:
A couple cats were a sight to see
You gotta leave to be with me
The cornerstone is right there you know
The neighbors have the best art show

Riddle Solution:
cats (near the Mountain Lions(plural) building)
leave (it's at an exit)
cornerstone (near a cornerstone)
art show (graffiti on nearby buildings)

Arkansas

Riddle:
The way The young one Thought to Play
Was below the bush on this fine day
Look Up and You Can See them rolling you know
Charlie says while looking below

Riddle Solution:
The young one (it's by the child mind statue)
Capital letters where they don't belong to show it's in the capital city of Arkansas
Look up, rolling (look up because there's a car over pass there)
Charlie says (Charlie says .....choo choo Charlie is a train and there are tracks above)

California

Riddle:
The man was over 80 years old and wore a nifty hat
The lady was 100 and her right tire was flat
A little left and a little down below was the coffee cup you know
The soggy birds loved the rain dancing on their toes

Clue 1:
The Candyman never liked Buttered Ppcrn jelly beans
Wet birds don't really fly as they aren't machines
May 30th is my birthday past tense
Dimes, Nichols, Quarters make perfect sense

Riddle Solution:
Over 80 (North of Interstate 80)(hat meant nothing)
Lady, 100 (Centennial plaza)
Right tire flat (Goodyear Bar is a town to the East/Right)
Left, down, coffee (Left and down is Maxwell-a coffee brand)
soggy birds (near the Feather River which is what the park is dedicated to)

Clue 1 Solution: (removed the O in popcorn because Oroville vs Orville(the popcorn company)
Wet birds (again relates to the Feather River)

May 30th past tense (in the past was Memorial day and it's on Memorial Dr)
(sense-cents...centennial park)

Colorado

Riddle:
Mark the rich man landed his best job yet
he could see his home from all around so there was no threat
park your car and out you go
read the words and look by Dennis' toe

Riddle Solution:
(Landmark-Mark Landed)
(castle rock can be seen from far away)
(rock park and near a parking lot)
(Plaque talks about Dennis who it was commemorating as a volunteer)

Connecticut

Riddle:
Blowing pages that do not cost
Look for time that seems so lost
In 1944 this really got big and wide
In 2013 the kids made this guide

Riddle Solution:
(blowing-WINDham)(there's the free library nearby)
(Time there is a time capsule there)
(there's a big tree there since 1944)

Delaware I

Riddle:
So The Gold Ticket is not here
may you email me your answer with no fear
you need to find the spot that I am
row over to me faster there is no dam
now tell me what is in front of the flag that you see
at the place you are, 6 letters I need
Email delaware@thegoldticket.com
I will tell the right answer where to find
The gold ticket was previously mine

Riddle Solution:
(ticket is under a rock that seems too hard to find so you will email us and we will tell you)
(it's near the water)
(it's an anchor)

Delaware II

Riddle:
Did the hippo cross the street and eat the gourmet food?
In the fall the farm is nice and puts you in a mood
The summer is the best of all, and you must go near there
Find a lonely tree with rocks so you can find it's glare

Clue 1:
The sporty shirt kept wanting to tell us some news
The big huge house is where we can snooze
It's old but two new, let's have some fun
It's cold now, but we love the sun.

Riddle Solution:
(because it's St. Augustine of Hippo is the road name)
(Augustine Inn is historic restaurant)
(the fall-August, Farm is the name of a road there)
(summer-you go to the beach)

Clue 2 Solution: (sporty shirt is New Jersey seen across the river, News is the smoke from the plant across the river in NJ giving off smoke signals)
(Big huge house is a castle-it's in New Castle County, Snooze is the Inn across the street)
(old but two new is New Jersey and New Castle)
(love the sun-beach)

Florida

Riddle:
The Alligator went to town, riding on a pony
He didn't like salt one bit at all, on his macaroni
Stare left, and pledge the spot
Woo Hoo you found the necklace worth a lot

Riddle Solution:
(used to be called Alligator) (Pony walks on a trail and this is on a famous trail)
(no salt because it's a lake)
(stare=stair left of them)(Pledge is the flag)

Georgia

Riddle:
I can I can find this middle first in a place
I can not sale it with an arms race
I do not want to fight as I am a happy space.

Clue 1:
How do you do,
How are you,
Hello

Clue 2:
Between the boards down below you can't see a thing.
Relief is in sight.
The spheres will sure sting.

Clue 3:
I'll sale you a treat
Just mention my name
and you'll get a good seat.

Riddle Solution:
(can can points to cannon, middle is where it is under the platform, first signifies the 1st exit) (sale=sail, there's a sail boat there, arms race=there is a rocket there)
(no fight, there's a sign that speaks of a battle)
(all the I's is for I-95, and there are 95 characters in the riddle)
Clue 1 Solution: (it's at a welcome center)
Clue 2 Solution: (it's under a deck platform) (relief-near bathrooms)(spheres-cannon balls)

Hawaii

Riddle:
Feeling bold is where I'll go
You won't feel bored don't you know
It's why you're here that you will see
make a wish and feel glee

Riddle Solution:
(bold-boulders)(bored/board)
(people go to Hawaii to surf)
(it's a fountain which is where people make wishes)

Idaho

Riddle:
Walk on the sidewalk as the stranger you are
You'll say mine oh mine and not walk too far
I'm yellow and roll as I go to and fro
I'm the power that takes you the way you want to go

Riddle Solution:
(Wallace means stranger)(it's near a sidewalk)
(Mining equipment)
(battery locomotive is yellow and rolls)
(power-battery)

Illinois

Riddle:
He laughed so hard it blew the fort down
Kids art was great to do in town
I was painted green way back in the day
Below the stones you'll find me today

Riddle Solution:
(blew a fort-Galesburg)
(kids art museum is there)
(train is green)
(it's below stones)

Indiana

Riddle:
I sang while I drifted into the dust
I rode my bike, so I wouldn't rust
I fell from a plane with 6 fine others
It's the RIGHT time for peace don't smoke my brothers

Riddle Solution:
(the song Broadway from the drifters)(covered in dust is sand)(it's on the corner of Broadway and W. Dune)
(it's near a bike and hiking trail)(you ride or walk on a trail for exercise)
(1933 a plane was bombed over Chesterton, IN and 7 people died)
(Calumet define is peace pipe)(Right-it's on the right side)

Iowa

Riddle:
No one would go with me, sad because the view
You were never second, the first time I saw you
You told me what you were, and how we came to be
I'm so lucky I found it beneath this growing tree

Clue 1:
The guys announced it loud and clear
the dust didn't get in their ears
I counted 244 gone by, oh my!
I was all alone with John and I

Riddle Solution:
(No would go with me-your independent)
(streets are first and second)
(It's telling you something...a letter-it's something you see that shows how we became independent)
(found=founding fathers)

Clue 1 Solution:
(244 years ago)
(dust in their ears-the old wigs they would wear had powder in them) (Independent is alone)(John-John Hancock)

Kansas

Riddle:
Oh shoot those specs are fine
I listen to the heavy metal all the time
A horse for a dollar I'd pay
I ate three while the legend runs a stray.

Riddle Solution:
(Oh for Oakley, specs are Oakley glasses)
(Heavy metal is bronze)
(Dollar is Bill)(horse he is riding a horse)
(Legend is legend of BB was born here)(83 is the road)(buffalo is a stray)

Kentucky

Riddle:
I was living in my own Pokémon land.
Eating some coconut chocolate bars and feeling grand
He couldn't stop chatting about how he loved Christmas time
The kids were all playing not far from the pine
Look under look over, it's a rock you want to see
A path is nearby take video for me

Riddle Solution:
(Pokémon land is Ash(character) land
(Coconut chocolate bars is mounds(indian mounds)
(under a pine tree)
(near a playground)

Louisiana

Riddle:
David was just 3 years old when he was on his way
He didn't know Flint but met him one day
Magnificent as her mom can know to sew
That doll sure loved to wear a rainbow

Riddle Solution:
(David went to California when he was 3-it's near the corner of California and Island)
(Captain Flint is the character in Treasure Island-it's near the corner of Island and California)
(Magnificent is the same as Grand)
(doll is Dolly and she'd wear a coat of many colors. This is Grand Cote)

Maine

Riddle:
He ain't swimming over there
A witty man who would be right here
5" deep in back it has sank
We'll show you a picture it is no prank

Riddle Solution:
(Have picture attached)
(Bryant Pond-he swimming)
(Whittman was the man who made the sculpture)(hear is hear on a phone)
(sank in ground)
(you prank call people)

Maryland

Riddle:
Shoeless Joe Jackson wouldn't play here
He'd be in the Midwest oh my dear
Go over to the boulder by the sign
Dig 4" down and you are fine!

Riddle Solution:
(it was at a park by the name of the Shoeless scandal)
(he was in Chicago)
(it's under a boulder)

Massachusetts

Riddle:
You might one day own this place you search
I don't think you're looking in a birch
First mow the hay it will take you all day
Owl says it's near 2 rocks, he won't lead you astray

Clue 1:
There's no owl here, but his home might be
We aren't in a cemetery as you can see
A compass can get you closer if you ask me
It's TIME to go look in a tree

Riddle Solution:
(Heritage means inherit land from family)
(it's not in a birch tree)
(hay is a meadow)(all day is long)
(owls are in knots in trees)(2 rocks are nearby)

Clue 1 Solution: (it's in a hole of a tree)
(people were going into a cemetery)
(A compass-East)
(two time capsules are near it and the gold ticket is in a tree)

Minnesota

Riddle:
At 20 he hit his prime, but one not ready to fight
Eight in the morning you come across this blaze of a site
Six men plus were not in lava where you're standing
Come to this strip by trees on road that is banding

Riddle Solution:

(20th prime is 71 and this is on route 71)
(The date of the battle is 1862. Each sentence has one of those numbers in it)
(Coulee is a lava flow)

Michigan

Riddle:
The gray heron knew where to go
a pie plate he loved to throw
He loved to eat with a fork
put a line in with a cork
Have fun and enjoy the dough

Riddle Solution:
(Rieger Park-Rieger means heron)
(pie plate-there are Frisbee golf is played there and frisbee started with pie plates being thrown)
(fork-this is known for the two waters forking at this location)
(cork-it's near water)

Mississippi

Riddle:
I never felt cheated from the man with the shoes
I forgot his name, but he was in the news
I got chills, they're multiplying
Be careful it could be electrifying.

Riddle Solution:
(cheated is fair park)(man shoes is Elvis-blue suede)
(forgot name-Alzheimer tree)(in the news-Elvis famous)
(multiplying-dog tags all above)
(electrifying-all metal tree with dog tags)

Missouri

Riddle:
I looked to see what was the time
I knew it would be fun, but I couldn't climb
Thomas didn't lie when he wrote the letter
His son was no everest or anything better

Riddle Solution:
(watch tower)
(You can't climb on the watch tower anymore)
(Thomas Jefferson-Jefferson County)(Thomas Jefferson invented the polygraph, which was not a lie detector, but rather a letter copying machine)
(it's in Sun Ridge Park-son and no Mt. Everest because it's a ridge or a hill-Hillsboro)

Montana

Riddle:
On my honor I will find this gold ticket now I promise
Orange you glad you don't need to share it with Thomas
Look under me and find my hiding spot
I'm not on the ground and that says a lot

Clue 1:
I'm on display yippee yay
The guy in the hat drives me all the way
I can't go no more, not even a bit
I'm hardy you see, and I don't quit

Riddle Solution:
(Laurel means honor)
(Orange is the color of the caboose)(Thomas is Thomas the train)

Clue 1 Solution:
(it's a display)
(guy in hat, a conductors hat)
(I can't go no more, it's a train that doesn't move anymore)
(Laurel and Hardy)(I think I can I think I can...the little engine that could)
(Ironically, we just noticed a Hardees is across the street)

Nebraska

Riddle:
The Great Bambino hit a home run
The Boone's loved to watch him for fun
The Dow Farm was a strange place to wow
I pulled over on the side of the road so I wouldn't hit a cow

Clue 1:
Did you enjoy the candy in my riddle
I'm now an adult and no longer little
Below the old sharpie you will see
Near the concrete is where I'll be

Clue 2:
Near some trees on the open highway
You'll find my story any time of day
I'm in a fake rock under a dusting of dirt
I drove almost to Tickertown wearing a skirt

Riddle Solution:
(Great Bambino is Babe Ruth and Babe Ruth was made by the
Curtiss Candy Company/ Curtis is the city its address is listed at)
(Boones are frontier people and this is in Frontier County)
(Dow Farm translates to Stockville
(it's at a pull over)

Clue 1 Solution: (Realize that candy is important in the original
riddle) (Sharpie-Marker)
Clue 2 Solution: (so people will know it's not in a city area) (it's a
sign with a story)
(Tickertown-Stockville)

Nevada

Riddle:
ring ring ring got a call from Clearwater I took
a car broke down so we read the book
I'm ok and THE fire is out
like the lights? They are flashing about

Clue 1:
Oh Dear don't have an emergency
X marks the spot in this treasure urgency
100 years ago stripes were in
Green ones though would make you win

Riddle Solution:
(call from Clearwater is area code 727 which is on the train)
(read the book is Chilton's auto manual and Mark Chilton moved
the tower)
(OK backwards is KO and THE is EL in Spanish for ELKO)
(the left side of riddle spells RAIL)

Clue 1 Solution: (Elk)(oh is O)(Emergency-by the emergency shut off) (X for railroad crossing)
(100 because it's at Chilton centennial)(Stripes are on the engine)
(Green because it's in Green Belt Park)

New Hampshire

Riddle:
Charlie gave me 3 quarters
David gave me 3 silver dimes
Penny could care less about the money
She just wanted to go for a ride

Clue 1:
Casey wears numbers you'll see when there
I'm on display for all to stare
Reading my riddle could give you my city
Treasure hunting is fun and enjoy this ditty

Clue 2:
The Grand old man's in town with silver hair
Loved to wheel his wife around in a chair
They could see themselves in the fork and spoon
Check out the ledge under the edge at noon

Clue 3:
I FALL from above and love little towns
My grandpa Randy left me 2 SILVER pounds
Look under the ledge near the wheel
A rock held me down, so no one will STEEL

Riddle Solution:
(Charlie is an engineer, 3 quarters is 75)
(3 silver dimes(30)
(Penny is 1 cent=7531 the train number)(silver-Gorham)
(ride-train)

Clue 1 Solution: (Casey is an engineer)
(Reading-Monopoly has a Reading Railroad)(Silver is sold by the Gorham Company)

Clue 2 Solution: (Grand Trunk)(Silver-Gorham silverware)
(wheel it's near a wheel)
(fork and spoon are silver)
(it's on the ledge under the edge)(trains come on specific times)

Clue 3 Solution: (Fall above is cascade)(Gorham is a smaller town)
(Randolph left is a town on the left of Gorham)(2 is the road that goes near there)(Silver is again Gorham)
(Steel because that's what the train is made of)

New Jersey

Riddle:
3 ducks were calm And 3 birds were cute
near this big rock is where you'll find the loot
Don't forget to take a fork to help cover up the school
Children will be screaming, happy time is absolutely cool

Riddle Solution:
(Address is 6 Tranquil…. add up the birds and you get 6 Tranquility. Also, the And is capitalized for And-dove-r…. so And-Dove(birds)
(Lackawanna means stream that forks)
(the sign tells you that school children cheered as their school was covered in rocks when the Lackawanna cut off was being constructed)

New Mexico

Riddle:
My watch told me to get my filling
A week is what I needed now so I was really thrilling
Ray was the one who showed me, the lead one he did love
Look under a little uppity spot, and 4" with a shove…..L(sorry, it didn't rhyme so well, but we're at the finishing line)

Clue 1:
There are 4 stages of riddle solving
Some folks thinking is evolving
Some want a riddle rider
My favorite is to be the canon hider

Clue 2:
Nick is coming over, make sure your shirts are pressed nice
I don't want you to stop believing that many paid a heavy price
All who said the ground might be frozen, remember treasure hunters must thrive
Dig 4" under the correct one, and you'll walk away with five
Nota-e photo of tha ectuel locetion would giva too much ewey.
Just esk Ray.

Riddle Solution:
(tooth of time is to signify the way to Santa Fe)
(you're traveling and it takes a week from that point to get to Santa Fe)
(Ray is for Reynaldo Rivera is the sculpture)
(uppity spot is a hoof being lifted, finishing line-journey's end and also horses race-finishing line)

Clue 1 Solution: (4 hooves)(stages-stagecoach) (Folk museum)(anthropology-evolving)
(rider-the horse hoof it's under has a rider)
(canon with 2 n's is a bone is in a horses leg)

Clue 2 Solution: (Nick is Santa)(shirts pressed with an iron and FE is for iron)
(don't stop believing is a Journey song-Journey's End)(heavy price paid for traveling on the trail) (Ray is Renaldo)

New York

Riddle:
To visit you must leave Little Arch yes in deed
Look up nearby and give it a read
Don't take too much time or change things so drastic
It's below the right post, you'll think it's fantastic

Clue 1:
Little Arch is really a cute guy
Come to this place and wave hello and hi
The side you will stop, when you are leaving
It's by a post not a tree and the doc's work can be deceiving

Clue 2:
HW+MW=AW
Don't drive through the red light, I care
The post is square and you're pulled off here
It's not in NYC or Long Island, so don't go there

Riddle Solution:
(little arch is the newest Windsor)
(read is the billboard)(change drastic-plastic surgery)

Clue 1 Solution:(Archie Windsor)
(at the welcome sign)
(doc deceiving because he changes things on a body from their natural state)

Clue 2 Solution:
(Harry Windsor +Megan Windsor=Archie Windsor)
(near a red light)
(it's near a pull off)

North Carolina

Riddle:
The crook in the tree carried the creatures all in black
I couldn't catch a break, nor could I slack.
If the coward bit me while I seek
I'd pee my pants before I shriek.

Clue 1:
It was 8:15 am when Carrie woke up and stretched as high as possible into the air
Her hair was all tangled and she used the wooden hair brush that hardly did a thing.

It was time for her little brother's game and she didn't really want to go.
So instead...she packed up the car, jumped in and went to find treasure!

Riddle Solution:
It's in a tree(crook of a tree), two small creatures(it's between two baseball fields-bats), Catch is a baseball term.
Coward is a hint towards cowardly lion and this is in Lyon's park
Pee my pants(near the bathroom), Shriek(the creatures are bats)

Clue 1 Solution: (Carrie=Cary)
(tangled=TANGLEwood)(wooden=tangleWOOD) (little brothers game-little league games played here)

North Dakota

Riddle:
Samuel and or Mark knew where to go
and Steve sang he did too.
They both would be very gentle
when they looked inside the flue

Riddle Solution:
(Mark Twain(real name Samuel) was a Steamboat operator(this is Steamboat Park)
(Steve singer(Fly like an Eagle Steve Miller)
(Flue(play on the word flew)

Ohio

Riddle:
Correct me if I'm wrong and give me an a instead of o.
I can't stop drinking in this place you maybe know
I face this special place, but there's no need to hike me
Find the pine tree near the car and 2" down you'll see

Riddle Solution:
(it's Worden instead of Warden)
(Hinkley like Hinkley and Schmidt the big water company)
(the faces that were carved along the trail)
(it's under the pine)

Oregon

Riddle:
Josie came upon this place, she's small and very cute
When she died she took pictures, and loved to honk and hoot
Go down by the post and move the gravel lightly
You will soon find me, I'm rather gold and brightly

Riddle Solution:
(in Josephine county)
(died-ghost, many people take photos of it , honk-road)

Pennsylvania

Riddle:
Jolly went as fast as can be
Make some friends with some leaves you see
I'm directly behind this cold metal bench
Dig down 4" but don't make a trench

Clue 1:
The man at the corner likes what you've grown
He doesn't like water in his eyes or he'll moan
Do they make bombs here in this nice place?
If you know The Candyman, he'd make this his base

Riddle Solution:
(Jolly-jolly GREEN giant-Green St.)(fast is race street)
(friends and leaves-friendship tree)

Clue 1 Solution: (farmer stand up wooden character that says
Farmer's Market)
(water in his eyes...Bath)
(Bath Bombs)
(The Candyman was in a bathtub on a cover of People Magazine)

Rhode Island

Riddle:
4" below is a special tree north you know
We have a picture to show you so you don't go too low
Oxygen creates future protection of roots as did this man
Don't play around too long or we'll call you Tarzan

Clue 1:
I didn't dunk a donut in my beer
It's not in a cemetery so don't go there.
Do you go North or South, only you will know
I think you'll like why this tree did grow

Clue 2:
Dale couldn't hurry up because she had already been drinking
Her horse didn't understand what she was thinking
The kids loved to play so don't go where they can not
Mosey on over to just the right spot

Riddle Solution:
(man=a man known for planting trees in the area)
(Miller Waite Evans Park=don't WAIT)

Clue 1 Solution: (Miller Waite Evans Park=Miller=beer)
(dunk=near a basketball court)
(North or South=It's North Providence)

Clue 3 Solution: (Dale=Evans)(hurry up=Waite)(drinking=Miller)
(horse relates to Dale Evans)(kids play=playground)

South Carolina

Riddle:
Walter Anderson's arm was sure red
Becoming an adult he might dread
His small simple house you will know
Move Northwest and a way, aglow

Riddle Solution:
Walterboro(name of airport), Anderson(was the name of the airport before that) Arm(Army)Red(Redtail)
It's off Cottageville Hwy. adult(Alt 17 which is not an adult)
Becoming an adult you might dread(being drafted)
directions(there's a compass-directions on the beacon-aglow-between the N and the W under a bush)

South Dakota

Riddle:
My mother's daughter was my best friend
She could lift an elephant till the very end
Round and round and round and round
No need to dig, as I'm not in the ground

Clue 1:
Time to make the donuts in a roundabout way
The horses love you and say neigh neigh
Watch for the star it's light and bold
Just like the ticket that's bright and gold

Riddle Solution:
(My Mother's daughter is my Sis)
(elephants are known to weigh a ton)
(it's in the 4th wheel from the back)

Clue 1 Solution: (donuts, because it's near Rosalie's bakery and near a roundabout street) (horses are in the middle of the roundabout)
(white start on tank)

Tennessee

Riddle:
The first girl on the scene wouldn't cross, but heard the screams of those we lost.
While eating gelatin and plastic ware and getting drunk over there.
Look straight down below the light.
No shovel needed to know you're right.

Clue 1:
Dolly won't help you
Neither will the Titanic
It's not a crowded place
Look for a rock type case

Clue 2:
No Pigeon, no Nashville,
not a crowded place.
You might not ever heard of me,
is what may be the case.

Riddle Solution:
(First girl=Eve St.)(Cross=Train Crossing)(those we lost=33
young guys lost their lives) (gelatin=Jellico)(plastic ware=near a
fork)(drunk=Tipple St)

Clue 1 Solution: (It's not in Pigeon Forge)
(it's in a quiet place)

Clue 2 Solution: (it's not in those places)
(such a small town)

Texas

Riddle:
Tom ate the big apple on his way
Walking over the small leak he goes today
Go two blocks and you will see
below some dirt is the key

Clue 1:
I'm not near El Paso or Amarillo now
I'm not very popular so don't say oh wow!
I'm near a crossing of water you see
Two Four Six really confuses me

Clue 2:
All good sons eat uno
School gave me a headache you know
Grab me a cookie on your way
You little hunter won't pay

Riddle Solution:
(Tom Sawyer at a Milam/Milum apple on his way to school-
Milam county)
(small leak is little river)
(2 blocks are the 2 monuments)

Clue 1 Solution: (Gause, Texas is not near there)
(low population)
(near a bridge)
(county road 264)

Clue 2 Solution:
(unscramble first letters to get town name Gause)
(School is college station)(headache is Temple)
(cookie is Milano)(little hunter is Little River and hunter is town
on other side which is Hearne)

Utah

Riddle:
The man told his oldest son to go grab his metal cane
Mr. Mr. Jones a teacher, liked to walk the little lane
Why he used such a tiny cup to quench his big ole thirst
He wasn't in the woods, so it made no sense at first

Riddle Solution:
(Caine's son's name is Enoch)(Metal because it's an iron workers
memorial)
(Mr. Mr. Jone's is John P Jone's and John Lee Jones who are
memorialized by this walking park)
(Tiny cup, it's near Dixie National Forest)

Vermont

Riddle:
The man stood 10' 6" tall
He was very troubled, and had moxy y'all
On his left his 4 friends grew
It's under a rock you'll start to accrue

Riddle Solution:
(10' = the sign by the bridge)
(trouble=bridge over troubled waters)(moxy=Moxley bridge)
(4 friends=4 trees next to each other)

Virginia I

Riddle:
I couldn't find a band of gold
as I go to the right of the cross
I tracked my vision to the middle
Find a crack and some rocks, don't piddle.

Clue 1:
He was a famous trumpet man
from out Chicago way.

Clue 2:
Johnny and Dan way back in 97
didn't cost them a dime
but it did, their friend Kevin.

Clue 3:
Tracks with no rail
Hope you get some mail
See exhibit or restore
So so big, you might adore

Clue 4:
The train might have brought you
You're about 12 minutes away
Find another method of transportation
Look in some rocks today

Riddle Solution:

RingGold is a town to the East of this location

Mt. Cross is to the West

Track(tanks are tracked vehicles)

Crack and rocks is where it is at that location under the rocks, but piddle(it's where you don't want to take long since it's near the building.

Clue 1 Solution: (military song and it's on 29B road. B for business)

Clue 2 Solution: (Johnny Cash sang a song Wreck of the old 97(happened in Danville) (the necklace is out front and not in the museum where it costs admission)

(Kevin went in and paid)

Clue 3 Solution: (tracks on a tank, not a train)

(you get mail when at war)

(The Tank museum has exhibits and restores tanks)

(Tanks are big)

Clue 4 Solution: (people were searching the train station because of the wreck of 97)

(that's how far from the train depot)

(tank instead of train)

(in the rocks in the planter)

Virginia II

Riddle:

A famous treasure guy in Santa Fe was he

He needed a candle burnt at both ends while drinking tea

Go look behind and you will surely find

A necklace that means so much to me

Riddle Solution:

(Famous treasure guy=Fenn)

(candle=Wick)

(look behind=behind the sign)

Washington

Riddle:
The Coo Coo Clock Xerus Could Vanish
Round and round the night visions I banish
Look up and remember them and that day
in a bush not far away is your play
Riddle Solution:
(CCCXCV stands for 395)
(Night Visions it's near Carousel of Dreams)
(Remember 9/11)

West Virginia I

Riddle:
They told us they're with us in strange ways you see
They told us to count and play together with me
I drive over there, up the street and even down
I know they are with me, when I play round and round

Clue 1:
Balance is what we all need in life.
Deciding who wins you wouldn't ask the wife.

Clue 2:
A black bird in the wild loves shiny things
He'll pick a rock that holds some bling
hidden in a small little shrub on the ground
Look for the words so that it can be found

Clue 3:
Don't make me sad in the big open space
Shuffle to the right when you see his face
A big rock is in front a little to the right
Enjoy your find it's out of sight.

Riddle Solution:
(Nash was schizophrenic)
(He was a mathematician)
(Nash is the name of a car(Nash Rambler))
(Nash won the Nobel Peace Prize for game theory)

Clue 1 Solution:
(Balance=Nash equilibrium theory)
(he was married and died with his wife)

Clue 2 Solution: (black bird=crow=Russell crow played Nash in the movie a beautiful mind) (words on the ground)

Clue 3 Solution: (BLUEfield=sad)(blueFIELD=big open space) (it was in a bush to the right of where his image is)

West Virginia II

Riddle:
You don't need to leave your village to find me
Even though you'll be outside to find thee
Not sure how far you'll need to drive
It's out there under the first archive

Riddle Solution:
(Hometown-don't leave village)
(first archive-Washington first president, archive is documented)

Wisconsin

Riddle:
Don't go in the water as it's too dark to see
look on the ground and you'll find me
I'm under some rocks, but don't climb at all
I have fed the needy and that's why I won't fall

Clue 1:
The forest is near the city I am in
You'll need to widen your circle to win
The wheat, the oats they might come here
Don't forget the berries, I'm no Shakespeare

Riddle Solution:
(water is river, dark is black)
(don't climb-there's a sign)
(memorial for people who fed the needy)(fall is Black River falls which is nearby)

Clue 1 Solution:
(Black River Forest is nearby)
(Millston is where grains would be processed)
(berry is a street nearby)

Wyoming

Riddle:
This town is such a treat and really really sweet
Daddy came upon it and was shy until you'd meet
The necklace is placed "low", a bit lower than your feet
Enjoy this veggie now, you'll really want to eat

Riddle Solution:
(the town processes beets into sugar) (CH Dad Worland is the founder) (Veggie is the beet)

CPSIA information can be obtained
at www.ICGtesting.com
Printed in the USA
LVHW021618240621
691048LV00009B/326

9 781736 236338